# TOTEM AND TABOO

## RESEMBLANCES BETWEEN THE PSYCHIC LIVES OF SAVAGES AND NEUROTICS

BY

## PROFESSOR DR. SIGMUND FREUD, LL.D.

Authorized English Translation
with Introduction by

### A. A. BRILL, Ph.B., M.D.

Asst. Prof. of Psychiatry, N. Y. Post Graduate Medical
School; Lecturer in Psychoanalvsis and Abnormal Psychology, New York University:
former Chief of Clinic of Psychiatry,
Columbia University

ISBN: 978-1-63182-880-5

Printed: March 2023

Published and Distributed By:
Lushena Books
607 Country Club Drive, Unit E
Bensenville, IL 60106
www.lushenabks.com

ISBN: 978-1-63182-880-5

# AUTHOR'S PREFACE

THE essays treated here appeared under the subtitle of this book in the first numbers of the periodical "Imago" edited by me. They represent my first efforts to apply view-points and results of psychoanalysis to unexplained problems of racial psychology. In method this book contrasts with that of W. Wundt and the works of the Zurich Psychoanalytic School. The former tries to accomplish the same object through assumptions ánd procedures from non-analytic psychology, while the latter follow the opposite course and strive to settle problems of individual psychology by referring to material of racial psychology.[1] I am pleased to say that the first stimulus for my own works came from these two sources.

I am fully aware of the shortcomings in these essays. I shall not touch upon those which are characteristic of first efforts at investigation. The others, however, demand a word of explana-

[1] Jung: Wandlungen und Symbole der Libido (Transformations and Symbols of the Libido) translated by Dr. Beatrice Hinkle under the title "The Psychology of the Unconscious," Moffat, Yard & Co., and "Principles of Psychoanalysis, Nervous and Mental Diseases," Monograph Series.

tion. The four essays which are here collected
will be of interest to a wide circle of educated people, but they can only be thoroughly understood
and judged by those who are really acquainted
with psychoanalysis as such. It is hoped that
they may serve as a bond between students of
ethnology, philology, folklore and of the allied
sciences, and psychoanalysts; they cannot, however, supply both groups the entire requisites for
such coöperation. They will not furnish the
former with sufficient insight into the new
psychological technique, nor will the psychoanalysts acquire through them an adequate command over the material to be elaborated. Both
groups will have to content themselves with whatever attention they can stimulate here and there
and with the hope that frequent meetings between them will not remain unproductive for science.

The two principle themes, totem and taboo,
which gave the name to this small book are not
treated alike here. The problem of taboo is pre-
sented more exhaustively, and the effort to solve
it is approached with perfect confidence. The
investigation of totemism may be modestly expressed as: "This is all that psychoanalytic study
can contribute at present to the elucidation of
the problem of totemism." This difference in
the treatment of the two subjects is due to the fact

that taboo still exists in our midst. To be sure, it is negatively conceived and directed to different contents, but according to its psychological nature, it is still nothing else than Kant's "Categorical Imperative," which tends to act compulsively and rejects all conscious motivations. On the other hand, totemism is a religio-social institution which is alien to our present feelings; it has long been abandoned and replaced by new forms. In the religions, morals, and customs of the civilized races of today it has left only slight traces, and even among those races where it is still retained, it has had to undergo great changes. The social and material progress of the history of mankind could obviously change taboo much less than totemism.

In this book the attempt is ventured to find the original meaning of totemism through its infantile traces, that is, through the indications in which it reappears in the development of our own children. The close connection between totem and taboo indicates the further paths to the hypothesis maintained here. And although this hypothesis leads to somewhat improbable conclusions, there is no reason for rejecting the possibility that it comes more or less near to the reality which is so hard to reconstruct.

# TRANSLATOR'S INTRODUCTION

WHEN one reviews the history of psychoanalysis[1] one finds that it had its inception in the study of morbid mental states. Beginning with the observation of hysteria and the other neuroses[2] Professor Freud gradually extended his investigations to normal psychology and evolved new concepts and new methods of study. The neurotic symptoms were no longer imaginary troubles the nature of which one could not grasp, but were conceived as mental and emotional maladjustments to one's environment. The stamp of degeneracy impressed upon neurotics by other schools of medicine was altogether eradicated. Deeper investigation showed conclusively that a person might become neurotic if subjected to certain environments, and that there was no definite dividing line between normal and abnormal. The hysterical symptoms, obsessions, doubts, phobias, as well as hallucinations of the insane, show the same mechanisms as those similar psy-

[1] "The History of the Psychoanalytic Movement," translated by A. A. Brill. Nervous and Mental Disease Monograph Series.
[2] "Selected Papers on Hysteria and Other Psychoneuroses," translated by A. A. Brill. Monograph Series.

chic structures which one constantly encounters
in normal persons in the form of mistakes in talk-
ing, reading, writing, forgetting,[3] dreams and
wit. The dream, always highly valued by the
populace, and as much despised by the educated classes, has a definite structure and meaning when subjected to analysis. Professor
Freud's monumental work, The Interpretation
of Dreams,[4] marked a new epoch in the history
of mental science. One might use the same
words in reference to his profound analysis of
wit.[5]

Faulty psychic actions, dreams and wit are
products of the unconscious mental activity, and
like neurotic or psychotic manifestations represent efforts at adjustment to one's environment.
The slip of the tongue shows that on account of
unconscious inhibitions the individual concerned
is unable to express his true thoughts; the dream
is a distorted or plain expression of those wishes
which are prohibited in the waking states, and the
witticism, owing to its veiled or indirect way of
expression, enables the individual to obtain
pleasure from forbidden sources. But whereas

[3] "The Psychopathology of Everyday Life," translated by A.
A. Brill. T. Fisher Unwin, London, and the Macmillan Co.,
N. Y.

[4] Translated by A. A. Brill, George Allen, and Unwin, London,
and the Macmillan Co., N. Y.

[5] "Wit and Its Relations to the Unconscious," translated by
A. A. Brill. Moffat, Yard and Co., N. Y.

dreams, witticisms, and faulty actions give evidences of inner conflicts which the individual overcomes, the neurotic or psychotic symptom is the result of a failure and represents a morbid adjustment.

The aforementioned psychic formations are therefore nothing but manifestations of the struggle with reality, the constant effort to adjust one's primitive feelings to the demands of civilization. In spite of all later development the individual retains all his infantile psychic struetures. Nothing is lost; the infantile wishes and primitive impulses can always be demonstrated in the grown up and on occasion can be brought back to the surface. In his dreams the normal person is constantly reviving his childhood, and the neurotic or psychotic individual merges back into a sort of psychic infantilism through his morbid productions. The unconscious mental activity which is made up of repressed infantile material forever strives to express itself. Whenever the individual finds it impossible to dominate the difficulties of the world of reality there is a regression to the infantile, and psychic disturbances ensue which are conceived as peculiar thoughts and acts. Thus the civilized adult is the result of his childhood or the sum total of his early impressions; psychoanalysis thus confirms the old saying: The child is father to the man.

It is at this point in the development of psychoanalysis that the paths gradually broadened until they finally culminated in this work. There were many indications that the childhood of the individual showed a marked resemblance to the primitive history or the childhood of races. The knowledge gained from dream analysis and phantasies,[6] when applied to the productions of racial phantasies, like myths and fairy tales, seemed to indicate that the first impulse to form myths was due to the same emotional strivings which produced dreams, fancies and symptoms.[7] Further study in this direction has thrown much light on our great cultural institutions, such as religion, morality, law and philosophy, all of which Professor Freud has modestly formulated in this volume and thus initiated a new epoch in the study of racial psychology.

I take great pleasure in acknowledging my indebtedness to Mr. Alfred B. Kuttner for the invaluable assistance he rendered in the translation of this work.

A. A. Brill.

[6] Freud: "Leonardo Da Vinci," translated by A. A. Brill. Moffat, Yard and Co., N. Y.

[7] Cf. the works of Abraham, Spielrein, Jung, and Rank.

# CONTENTS

# TOTEM AND TABOO

## CHAPTER I

### THE SAVAGE'S DREAD OF INCEST

PRIMITIVE man is known to us by the stages of development through which he has passed: that is, through the inanimate monuments and implements which he has left behind for us, through our knowledge of his art, his religion and his attitude towards life, which we have received either directly or through the medium of legends, myths and fairy-tales; and through the remnants of his ways of thinking that survive in our own manners and customs. Moreover, in a certain sense he is still our contemporary: there are people whom we still consider more closely related to primitive man than to ourselves, in whom we therefore recognize the direct descendants and representatives of earlier man. We can thus judge the so-called savage and semi-savage races; their psychic life assumes a peculiar interest for us, for we can recognize in their psychic life a well-preserved, early stage of our own development.

If this assumption is correct, a comparison of the "Psychology of Primitive Races" as taught by folklore, with the psychology of the neurotic as it has become known through psychoanalysis, will reveal numerous points of correspondence and throw new light on subjects that are more or less familiar to us.

For outer as well as for inner reasons, I am choosing for this comparison those tribes which have been described by ethnographists as being most backward and wretched: the aborigines of the youngest continent, namely Australia, whose fauna has also preserved for us so much that is archaic and no longer to be found elsewhere.

The aborigines of Australia are looked upon as a peculiar race which shows neither physical nor linguistic relationship with its nearest neighbors, the Melanesian, Polynesian and Malayan races. They do not build houses or permanent huts; they do not cultivate the soil or keep any domestic animals except dogs; and they do not even know the art of pottery. They live exclusively on the flesh of all sorts of animals which they kill in the chase, and on the roots which they dig. Kings or chieftains are unknown among them, and all communal affairs are decided by the elders in assembly. It is quite doubtful whether they evince any traces of religion in the form of worship of higher beings. The tribes living in the interior who have to contend with the greatest vicissitudes of life owing to a scarcity of water, seem in every way more primitive than those who live near the coast.

We surely would not expect that these poor, naked cannibals should be moral in their sex life according to our ideas, or that they should have imposed a high degree of restriction upon their sexual impulses. And yet we learn that they have considered it their duty to exercise the most searching care and the most painful rigor in guarding against incestuous sexual relations. In fact their whole social organization seems to serve this object or to have been brought into relation with its attainment.

Among the Australians the system of *Totemism* takes the place of all religious and social institutions. Australian tribes are divided into smaller *septs* or clans, each taking the name of its *totem*. Now what is a totem? As a rule it is an animal, either edible and harmless, or dangerous and feared; more rarely the totem is a plant or a force of nature (rain, water), which stands in a peculiar relation to the whole clan. The totem is first of all the tribal ancestor of the clan, as well as its tutelary spirit and protector; it sends oracles and, though otherwise dangerous, the totem knows and spares its children. The members of a totem are therefore under a sacred obligation not to kill (destroy) their totem, to abstain from eating its meat or from any other enjoyment of it. Any violation of these prohibitions is automatically punished. The character of a totem is inherent not only in a single animal or a single being but in all the members of the species. From time to time festivals are held at which the members of a totem represent or imitate, in ceremonial dances, the movements and characteristics of their totems.

The totem is hereditary either through the maternal or the paternal line; (maternal transmission probably always preceded and was only later supplanted by the paternal). The attachment to a totem is the foundation of all the social obligations of an Australian: it extends on the one hand beyond the tribal relationship, and on the other hand it supersedes consanguinous relationship.[1]

The totem is not limited to district or to locality; the members of a totem may live separated from one another and on friendly terms with adherents of other totems.[2]

[1] Frazer, "Totemism and Exogamy," Vol. I, p. 53. "The totem bond is stronger than the bond of blood or family in the modern sense."

[2] This very brief extract of the totemic system cannot be left without some elucidation and without discussing its limitations. The name Totem or Totam was first learned from the North American Indians by the Englishman, J. Long, in 1791. The subject has gradually acquired great scientific interest and has called forth a copious literature. I refer especially to "Totemism and Exogamy" by J. G. Frazer, 4 vols., 1910, and the books

And now, finally, we must consider that peculiarity of the totemic system which attracts the interest of the psychoanalyst. Almost everywhere the totem prevails there also exists the

and articles of Andrew Lang ("The Secret of Totem," 1905). The credit for having recognized the significance of totemism for the ancient history of man belongs to the Scotchman, J. Ferguson MacLennan (*Fortnightly Review*, 1869–70). Exterior to Australia, totemic institutions were found and are still observed among North American Indians, as well as among the races of the Polynesian Islands group, in East India, and in a large part of Africa. Many traces and survivals otherwise hard to interpret lead to the conclusion that totemism also once existed among the aboriginal Aryan and Semitic races of Europe, so that many investigators are inclined to recognize in totemism a necessary phase of human development through which every race has passed.

How then did prehistoric man come to acquire a totem; that is, how did he come to make his descent from this or that animal foundation of his social duties and, as we shall hear, of his sexual restrictions as well? Many different theories have been advanced to explain this, a review of which the reader may find in Wundt's "Volkerpsychologie" (Vol. II, Mythus und Religion).

I promise soon to make the problem of totemism a subject of special study in which an effort will be made to solve it by applying the psychoanalytic method. (Cf. The fourth chapter of this work.)

Not only is the theory of totemism controversial, but the very facts concerning it are hardly to be expressed in such general statements as were attempted above. There is hardly an assertion to which one would not have to add exceptions and contradictions. But it must not be forgotten that even the most primitive and conservative races are, in a certain sense, old, and have a long period behind them during which whatsoever was aboriginal with them has undergone much development and distortion. Thus among those races who still evince it, we find totemism today in the most manifold states of decay and disintegration; we observe that fragments of it have passed over to other social and religious institutions; or it may exist in fixed forms but far removed from its original nature. The difficulty then consists in the fact that it is not altogether easy to decide what in the actual conditions is to be taken as a faithful copy of the significant past and what is to be considered as a secondary distortion of it.

law thát *the members of the same totem are not allowed to enter into sexual relations with each other; that is, that they cannot marry each other.* This represents the *exogamy* which is associated with the totem.

This sternly maintained prohibition is very remarkable. There is nothing to account for it in anything that we have hitherto learned from the conception of the totem or from any of its attributes; that is, we do not understand how it happened to enter the system of totemism. We are therefore not astonished if some investigators simply assume that at first exogamy—both as to its origin and to its meaning—had nothing to do with totemism, but that it was added to it at some time without any deeper association, when marriage restrictions proved necessary. However that may be, the association of totemism and exogamy exists, and proves to be very strong.

Let us elucidate the meaning of this prohibition through further discussion.

a) The violation of the prohibition is not left to what is, so to speak, an automatic punishment, as is the case with other violations of the prohibitions of the totem (e.g., not to kill the totem animal), but is most energetically avenged by the whole tribe as if it were a question of warding off a danger that threatens the community as a whole or a guilt that weighs upon all. A few

sentences from Frazer's book [3] will show how
seriously such trespasses are treated by these
savages who, according to our standard, are
otherwise very immoral.

"In Australia the regular penalty for sexual
intercourse with a person of a forbidden clan is
death. It matters not whether the woman is
of the same local group or has been captured in
war from another tribe; a man of the wrong clan
who uses her as his wife is hunted down and
killed by his clansmen, and so is the woman;
though in some cases, if they succeed in eluding
capture for a certain time, the offense may be
condoned. In the Ta-Ta-thi tribe, New South
Wales, in the rare cases which occur, the man is
killed, but the woman is only beaten or speared,
or both, till she is nearly dead; the reason given
for not actually killing her being that she was
probably coerced. Even in casual amours the
clan prohibitions are strictly observed; any violations of these prohibitions ' are regarded with
the utmost abhorrence and are punished by
death ' (Howitt)."

b)   As the same severe punishment is also
meted out for temporary love affairs which have
not resulted in childbirth, the assumption of
other motives, perhaps of a practical nature, becomes improbable.

[3] Frazer, l. c. p. 54.

c)  As the totem is hereditary and is not changed by marriage, the results of the prohibition, for instance in the case of maternal heredity, are easily perceived.  If, for example, the man belongs to a clan with the totem of the Kangaroo and marries a woman of the Emu totem, the children, both boys and girls, are all Emu.  According to the totem law incestuous relations with his mother and his sister, who are Emu like himself, are therefore made impossible for a son of this marriage.[4]

d)  But we need only a reminder to realize that the exogamy connected with the totem accomplishes more; that is, aims at more than the prevention of incest with the mother or the sisters. It also makes it impossible for the man to have sexual union with all the women of his own group, with a number of females, therefore, who are not consanguinously related to him, by treating all these women like blood relations.  The psychological justification for this extraordinary restriction, which far exceeds anything comparable to

[4] But the father, who is a Kangaroo, is free—at least under this prohibition—to commit incest with his daughters, who are Emu. In the case of paternal inheritance of the totem the father would be Kangaroo as well as the children; then incest with the daughters would be forbidden to the father and incest with the mother would be left open to the son.  These consequences of the totem prohibition seem to indicate that the maternal inheritance is older than the paternal one, for there are grounds for assuming that the totem prohibitions are directed first of all against the incestuous desires of the son.

it among civilized races, is not, at first, evident.
All we seem to understand is that the rôle of the
totem (the animal) as ancestor is taken very seriously. Everybody descended from the same
totem is consanguinous; that is, of one family;
and in this family the most distant grades of relationship are recognized as an absolute obstacle
to sexual union.

Thus these savages reveal to us an unusually
high grade of incest dread or incest sensitiveness,
combined with the peculiarity, which we do not
very well understand, of substituting the totem
relationship for the real blood relationship. But
we must not exaggerate this contradiction too
much, and let us bear in mind that the totem
prohibitions include real incest as a special case.

In what manner the substitution of the totem
group for the actual family has come about remains a riddle, the solution of which is perhaps
bound up with the explanation of the totem itself. Of course it must be remembered that with
a certain freedom of sexual intercourse, extending beyond the limitations of matrimony, the
blood relationship, and with it also the prevention
of incest, becomes so uncertain that we cannot
dispense with some other basis for the prohibition.
It is therefore not superfluous to note that the
customs of Australians recognize social conditions and festive occasions at which the exclusive

conjugál right of a man to a woman is violated.

The linguistic custom of these tribes, as well as of most totem races, reveals a peculiarity which undoubtedly is pertinent in this connection. For the designations of relationship of which they make use do not take into consideration the relation between two individuals, but between an individual and his group; they belong, according to the expression of L. H. Morgan, to the "classifying" system. That means that a man calls not only his begetter "father" but also every other man who, according to the tribal regulations, might have married his mother and thus become his father; he calls "mother" not only the woman who bore him but also every other woman who might have become his mother without violation of the tribal laws; he calls "brothers" and "sisters" not only the children of his real parents, but also the children of all the persons named who stand in the parental group relation with him, and so on. The kinship names which two Australians give each other do not, therefore, necessarily point to a blood relationship between them, as they would have to according to the custom of our language; they signify much more the social than the physical relations. An approach to this classifying system is perhaps to be found in our nursery, when the child is induced to greet every male and female friend of the parents as "uncle" and "aunt," or it may be found in a transferred sense when we speak of "Brothers in Apollo," or "Sisters in Christ."

The explanation of this linguistic custom, which seems so strange to us, is simple if looked upon as a remnant and indication of those marriage institutions which the Rev. L. Fison has called "group marriage," characterized by a number of men exercising conjugal rights over a number of women. The children of this group marriage would then rightly look upon each other as brothers and sisters although not born of the same mother, and would take all the men of the group for their fathers.

Although a number of authors, as, for instance, B. Westermarck in his "History of Human Marriage," [5] oppose the conclusions which others have drawn from the existence of group-relationship names, the best authorities on the Australian savages are agreed that the classificatory relationship names must be considered as survivals from the period of group marriages. And, according to Spencer and Gillen,[6] a certain form of group marriage can be established as still existing to-day among the tribes of the Urabunna and the Dieri. Group marriage therefore preceded individual marriage among these races

[5] Second edition, 1902.
[6] "The Native Tribes of Central Australia," London, 1899.

and did not disappear without leaving distinct traces in language and custom.

But if we replace individual marriage, we can then grasp the apparent excess of cases of incest shunning which we have met among these same races. The totem exogamy, or prohibition of sexual intercourse between members of the same clan, seemed the most appropriate means for the prevention of group incest; and this totem exogamy then became fixed and long survived its original motivation.

Although we believe that we understand the motives of the marriage restrictions among the Australian savages, we have still to learn that the actual conditions reveal a still more bewildering complication. For there are only few tribes in Australia which show no other prohibition besides the totem barrier. Most of them are so organized that they fall into two divisions which have been called marriage classes, or phratries. Each of these marriage groups is exogamous and includes a majority of totem groups. Usually each marriage group is again divided into two sub-classes (sub-phratries), and the whole tribe is therefore divided into four classes; the sub-classes thus standing between the phratries and the totem groups.

The typical and often very intricate scheme

of organization of an Australian tribe therefore looks as follows:

The twelve totem groups are brought under four subclasses and two main classes. All the divisions are exogamous.[7] The subclass c forms an exogamous unit with e, and the subclass d with f. The success or the tendency of these arrangements is quite obvious; they serve as a further restriction on the marriage choice and on sexual freedom. If there were only these twelve totem groups—assuming the same number of people in each group—every member of a group would have $^{11}/_{12}$ of all the women of the tribe to choose from. The existence of the two phratries reduces this number to $^{6}/_{12}$ or $\frac{1}{2}$; a man of the totem a can only marry a woman from the groups 1 to 6. With the introduction of the two subclasses the selection sinks to $^{3}/_{12}$ or $\frac{1}{4}$; a man of

[7] The number of totems is arbitrarily chosen.

the totem *a* must limit his marriage choice to the woman of the totems 4, 5, 6.

The historical relations of the marriage classes —of which there are found as many as eight in some tribes—are quite unexplained. We only see that these arrangements seek to attain the same object as the totem exogamy, and even strive for more. But whereas the totem exogamy makes the impression of a sacred statute which sprang into existence, no one knows how, and is therefore a custom, the complicated institutions of the marriage classes, with their subdivisions and the conditions attached to them, seem to spring from legislation with a definite aim in view. They have perhaps taken up afresh the task of incest prohibition because the influence of the totem was on the wane. And while the totem system is, as we know, the basis of all other social obligations and moral restrictions of the tribe, the importance of the phratries generally ceases when the regulation of the marriage choice at which they aimed has been accomplished.

In the further development of the classification of the marriage system there seems to be a tendency to go beyond the prevention of natural and group incest, and to prohibit marriage between more distant group relations, in a manner similar to the Catholic church, which extended the marriage prohibitions always in force for brother and sisters, to cousins, and invented for them the grades of spiritual kinship.[8]

It would hardly serve our purpose to go into the extraordinarily intricate and unsettled discussion concerning the origin and significance of the marriage classes, or to go more deeply into their relation to totemism. It is sufficient for our purposes to point out the great care expended by the Australians as well as by other savage people to prevent incest.[9] We must say that these savages are even more sensitive to incest than we, perhaps because they are more subject to temptations than we are, and hence require more extensive protection against it.

But the incest dread of these races does not content itself with the creation of the institutions described, which, in the main, seem to be directed against group incest. We must add a series of "customs" which watch over the individual behavior to near relatives in our sense, which are maintained with almost religious severity and of whose object there can hardly be any doubt. These customs or custom prohibitions may be called "avoidances." They spread far beyond

8 Article "Totemism" in Encyclopedia Britannica, eleventh edition, 1911 (A. Lang).

9 Storfer has recently drawn special attention to this point in his monograph: "Parricide as a Special Case. Papers on Applied Psychic Investigation," No. 12, Vienna, 1911.

the Australian totem races. But here again I must ask the reader to be content with a fragmentary excerpt from the abundant material.

Such restrictive prohibitions are directed in Melanesia against the relations of boys with their mothers and sisters. Thus, for instance, on Lepers Island, one of the New Hebrides, the boy leaves his maternal home at a fixed age and moves to the "clubhouse," where he then regularly sleeps and takes his meals. He may still visit his home to ask for food; but if his sister is at home he must go away before he has eaten; if no sister is about he may sit down to eat near the door. If brother and sister meet by chance in the open, she must run away or turn aside and conceal herself. If the boy recognizes certain footprints in the sand as his sister's he is not to follow them, nor is she to follow his. He will not even mention her name and will guard against using any current word if it forms part of her name. This avoidance, which begins with the ceremony of puberty, is strictly observed for life. The reserve between mother and son increases with age and generally is more obligatory on the mother's side. If she brings him something to eat she does not give it to him herself but puts it down before him, nor does she address him in the familiar manner of mother and son, but uses the formal address. Similar customs obtain in New

Caledonia. If brother and sister meet, she flees into the bush and he passes by without turning his head toward her.[10]

On the Gazella Peninsula in New Britain a sister, beginning with her marriage, may no longer speak with her brother, nor does she utter his name but designates him by means of a circumlocution.[11]

In New Mecklenburg some cousins are subject to such restrictions, which also apply to brothers and sisters. They may neither approach each other, shake hands, nor give each other presents, though they may talk to each other at a distance of several paces. The penalty for incest with a sister is death through hanging.[12]

These rules of avoidance are especially severe in the Fiji Islands where they concern not only consanguinous sisters but group sisters as well. To hear that these savages hold sacred orgies in which persons of just these forbidden degrees of kinship seek sexual union would seem still more peculiar to us, if we did not prefer to make use of this contradiction to explain the prohibition instead of being astonished at it.[13]

[10] R. H. Codrington, "The Melanesians," also Frazer: "Totemism and Exogamy," Vol. I, p. 77.

[11] Frazer, l. c. II, p. 124, according to Kleintischen: The Inhabitants of the Coast of the Gazelle Peninsula.

[12] Frazer, l. c. II, p. 131, according to P. G. Peckel in Anthropes, 1908.

[13] Fraser, l. c. II, p. 147, according to the Rev. L. Fison.

Among the Battas of Sumatra these laws of
avoidance affect all near relationships. For instance, it would be most offensive for a Battan
to accompany his own sister to an evening party.
A brother will feel most uncomfortable in the
company of his sister even when other persons are
also present. If either comes into the house, the
other prefers to leave. Nor will a father remain
alone in the house with his daughter any more
than the mother with her son. The Dutch missionary who reported these customs added that
unfortunately he had to consider them well
founded. It is assumed without question by
these races that a man and a woman left
alone together will indulge in the most extreme intimacy, and as they expect all kinds
of punishments and evil consequences from
consanguinous intercourse they do quite right
to avoid all temptations by means of such prohibitions.[14]

Among the Barongos in Delagoa Bay, in
Africa, the most rigorous precautions are directed, curiously enough, against the sister-in-
law, the wife of the brother of one's own wife.
If a man meets this person who is so dangerous
to him, he carefully avoids her. He does not
dare to eat out of the same dish with her; he
speaks only timidly to her, does not dare to enter

[14] Frazer, l. c. II, p. 189.

her hut, and greets her only with a trembling voice.[15]

Among the Akamba (or Wakamba) in British East Africa, a law of avoidance is in force which one would have expected to encounter more frequently. A girl must carefully avoid her own father between the time of her puberty and her marriage. She hides herself if she meets him on the street and never attempts to sit down next to him, behaving in this way right up to her engagement. But after her marriage no further obstacle is put in the way of her social intercourse with her father.[16]

The most widespread and strictest avoidance, which is perhaps the most interesting one for civilized races, is that which restricts the social relations between a man and his mother-in-law. It is quite general in Australia, but it is also in force among the Melanesian, Polynesian and Negro races of Africa as far as the traces of totemism and group relationship reach, and probably further still. Among some of these races similar prohibitions exist against the harmless social intercourse of a wife with her father-in-law, but these are by far not so constant or so serious. In a few cases both parents-in-law become objects of avoidance.

[15] Frazer, l. c. II, p. 388, according to Junod.
[16] Frazer, l. c. II, p. 424.

As we are less interested in the ethnographic dissemination than in the substance and the purpose of the mother-in-law avoidance, I will here also limit myself to a few examples. On the Banks Island these prohibitions are very severe and painfully exact. A man will avoid the proximity of his mother-in-law as she avoids his. If they meet by chance on a path, the woman steps aside and turns her back until he is passed, or he does the same.

In Vanna Lava (Port Patterson) a man will not even walk behind his mother-in-law along the beach until the rising tide has washed away the trace of her foot-steps. But they may talk to each other at a certain distance. It is quite out of the question that he should ever pronounce the name of his mother-in-law, or she his.[17]

On the Solomon Islands, beginning with his marriage, a man must neither see nor speak with his mother-in-law. If he meets her he acts as if he did not know her and runs away as fast as he can in order to hide himself.[18]

Among the Zulu Kaffirs custom demands that a man should be ashamed of his mother-in-law and that he should do everything to avoid her company. He does not enter a hut in which she

17 Frazer, l. c. II, p. 76.
18 Frazer, l. c. II, p. 113, according to C. Ribbe: "Two Years among the Cannibals of the Solomon Islands," 1905.

is, and when they meet he or she goes aside, she perhaps hiding behind a bush while he holds his shield before his face.  If they cannot avoid each other and the woman has nothing with which to cover herself, she at least binds a bunch of grass around her head in order to satisfy the ceremonial requirements.  Communication between them must either be made through a third person or else they may shout at each other at a considerable distance if they have some barrier between them as, for instance, the enclosure of a kraal. Neither may utter the other's name.[19]

Among the Basogas, a negro tribe living in the region of the Nile sources, a man may talk to his mother-in-law only if she is in another room of the house and is not visible to him.  Moreover, this race abominates incest to such an extent as not to let it go unpunished even among domestic animals.[20]

Whereas all observers have interpreted the purpose and meaning of the avoidances between near relatives as protective measures against incest, different interpretations have been given for those prohibitions which concern the relationship with the mother-in-law.  It was quite incomprehensible why all these races should manifest such great fear of temptation on the part of the man

[19] Frazer, l. c. II, p. 385.
[20] Frazer, l. c. II, p. 461.

for an elderly woman, old enough to be his mother.[21]

The same objection was also raised against the conception of Fison who called attention to the fact that certain marriage class systems show a gap in that they make marriage between a man and his mother-in-law theoretically not impossible and that a special guarantee was therefore necessary to guard against this possibility.

Sir J. Lubbock, in his book "The Origin of Civilization," traces back the behavior of the mother-in-law toward the son-in-law to the former "marriage by capture." "As long as the capture of women actually took place, the indignation of the parents was probably serious enough. When nothing but symbols of this form of marriage survived, the indignation of the parents was also symbolized and this custom continued after its origin had been forgotten." Crawley has found it easy to show how little this tentative explanation agrees with the details of actual observation.

E. B. Tylor thinks that the treatment of the son-in-law on the part of the mother-in-law is nothing more than a form of "cutting" on the part of the woman's family. The man counts as a stranger, and this continues until the first child is born. But even if no account is taken of cases

[21] V. Crawley: "The Mystic Rose," London, 1902, p. 405.

in which this last condition does not remove the prohibition, this explanation is subject to the objection that it does not throw any light on the custom dealing with the relation between mother-in-law and son-in-law, thus overlooking the sexual factor, and that it does not take into account the almost sacred loathing which finds expression in the laws of avoidance.[22]

A Zulu woman who was asked about the basis for this prohibition showed great delicacy of feeling in her answer: "It is not right that he should see the breasts which nursed his wife." [23]

It is known that also among civilized races the relation of son-in-law and mother-in-law belongs to one of the most difficult sides of family organization. Although laws of avoidance no longer exist in the society of the white races of Europe and America, much quarreling and displeasure would often be avoided if they did exist and did not have to be reëstablished by individuals. Many a European will see an act of high wisdom in the laws of avoidance which savage races have established to preclude any understanding between two persons who have become so closely related. There is hardly any doubt that there is something in the psychological situation of

22 Crawley, l. c. p. 407.
23 Crawley, l. c. p. 401, according to Leslie: "Among the Zulus and Amatongas," 1875.

mother-in-law and son-in-law which furthers hostilities between them and renders living together difficult. The fact that the witticisms of civilized races show such a preference for this very mother-in-law theme seems to me to point to the fact that the emotional relations between mother-in-law and son-in-law are controlled by components which stand in sharp contrast to each other. I mean that the relation is really "ambivalent," that is, it is composed of conflicting feelings of tenderness and hostility.

A certain part of these feelings is evident. The mother-in-law is unwilling to give up the possession of her daughter; she distrusts the stranger to whom her daughter has been delivered, and shows a tendency to maintain the dominating position, to which she became accustomed at home. On the part of the man, there is the determination not to subject himself any longer to any foreign will, his jealousy of all persons who preceded him in the possession of his wife's tenderness, and, last but not least, his aversion to being disturbed in his illusion of sexual overvaluation. As a rule such a disturbance emanates for the most part from his mother-in-law who reminds him of her daughter through so many common traits but who lacks all the charm of youth, such as beauty and that psychic spontaneity which makes his wife precious to him.

The knowledge of hidden psychic feelings which psychoanalytic investigation of individuals has given us, makes it possible to add other motives to the above. Where the psychosexual needs of the woman are to be satisfied in marriage and family life, there is always the danger of dissatisfaction through the premature termination of the conjugal relation, and the monotony in the wife's emotional life. The ageing mother protects herself against this by living through the lives of her children by identifying herself with them and making their emotional experiences her own. Parents are said to remain young with their children, and this is, in fact, one of the most valuable psychic benefits which parents derive from their children. Childlessness thus eliminates one of the best means to endure the necessary resignation imposed upon the individual through marriage. This emotional identification with the daughter may easily go so far with the mother that she also falls in love with the man her daughter loves, which leads, in extreme cases, to severe forms of neurotic ailments on account of the violent psychic resistance against this emotional predisposition. At all events the tendency to such infatuation is very frequent with the mother-in-law, and either this infatuation itself or the tendency opposed to it joins the conflict of contending forces in the psyche of the mother-in-law. Very often it is just this harsh and sadistic component of the love emotion which is turned against the son-in-law in order better to suppress the forbidden tender feelings.

The relation of the husband to his mother-in-law is complicated through similar feelings which, however, spring from other sources. The path of object selection has normally led him to his love object through the image of his mother and perhaps of his sister; in consequence of the incest barriers his preference for these two beloved persons of his childhood has been deflected and he is then able to find their image in strange objects. He now sees the mother-in-law taking the place of his own mother and of his sister's mother, and there develops a tendency to return to the primitive selection, against which everything in him resists. His incest dread demands that he should not be reminded of the genealogy of his love selection; the actuality of his mother-in-law, whom he had not known all his life like his mother so that her picture can be preserved unchanged in his unconscious, facilitates this rejection. An added mixture of irritability and animosity in his feelings leads us to suspect that the mother-in-law actually represents an incest temptation for the son-in-law, just as it not infrequently happens that a man falls in love with his subsequent

mother-in-law before his inclination is transferred to her daughter.

I see no objection to the assumption that it is
júst this incestuous factor of the relationship
which motivates the avoidance between son- and
mother-in-law among savages. Among the explanations for the "avoidances" which these
primitive races observe so strictly, we would
therefore give preference to the opinion originally expressed by Fison, who sees nothing in these
regulations but a protection against possible incest. This would also hold good for all the
other avoidances between those related by blood
or by marriage. There is only one difference,
namely, in the first case the incest is direct, so
that the purpose of the prevention might be conscious; in the other case, which includes the
mother-in-law relation, the incest would be a
phantasy temptation brought about by unconscious intermediary links.

We have had little opportunity in this exposition to show that the facts of folk psychology can
be seen in a new light through the application
of the psychoanalytic point of view, for the incest dread of savages has long been known as
such, and is in need of no further interpretation. What we can add to the further appreciation of incest dread is the statement that it is a

subtle infantile trait and is in striking agreement with the psychic life of the neurotic. Psychoanalysis has taught us that the first object selection of the boy is of an incestuous nature and that it is directed to the forbidden objects, the mother and the sister; psychoanalysis has taught us also the methods through which the maturing individual frees himself from these incestuous attractions. The neurotic, however, regularly presents to us a piece of psychic infantilism; he has either not been able to free himself from the childlike conditions of psychosexuality, or else he has returned to them (inhibited development and regression). Hence the incestuous fixations of the libido still play or again are playing the main rôle in his unconscious psychic life. We have gone so far as to declare that the relation to the parents instigated by incestuous longings, is the central complex of the neurosis. This discovery of the significance of incest for the neurosis naturally meets with the most general incredulity on the part of the grown-up, normal man; a similar rejection will also meet the researches of Otto Rank, which show in even larger scope to what extent the incest theme stands in the center of poetical interest and how it forms the material of poetry in countless variations and distortions. We are forced to believe that such a rejection is above all the product of man's deep aversion

to his former incest wishes which have since suc-
cumbed to repression. It is therefore of importance to us to be able to show that man's incest wishes, which later are destined to become
unconscious, are still felt to be dangerous by savage races who consider them worthy of the most
severe defensive measures.

# CHAPTER II

TABOO AND THE AMBIVALENCE OF EMOTIONS

1

TABOO is a Polynesian word, the translation of which provides difficulties for us because we no longer possess the idea which it connotes. It was still current with the ancient Romans: their word "sacer" was the same as the taboo of the Polynesians. The "ἄγος" of the Greeks and the "Kodaush" of the Hebrews must also have signified the same thing which the Polynesians express through their word taboo and what many races in America, Africa (Madagascar), North and Central Asia express through analogous designations.

For us the meaning of taboo branches off into two opposite directions. On the one hand it means to us sacred, consecrated: but on the other hand it means, uncanny, dangerous, forbidden, and unclean. The opposite for taboo is designated in Polynesian by the word *noa* and signifies something ordinary and generally accessible. Thus something like the concept of reserve inheres in taboo; taboo expresses itself essentially in prohibitions and restrictions. Our combination of "holy dread" would often express the meaning of taboo.

The taboo restrictions are different from religious or moral prohibitions. They are not traced to a commandment of a god but really they themselves impose their own prohibitions; they are differentiated from moral prohibitions by failing to be included in a system which declares abstinences in general to be necessary and gives reasons for this necessity. The taboo prohibitions lack all justification and are of unknown origin. Though incomprehensible to us they are taken as a matter of course by those who are under their dominance.

Wundt[1] calls taboo the oldest unwritten code of law of humanity. It is generally assumed that taboo is older than the gods and goes back to the pre-religious age.

As we are in need of an impartial presentation of the subject of taboo before subjecting it to psychoanalytic consideration I shall now cite an excerpt from the article "Taboo" in the Encyclopedia Britannica written by the anthropologist Northcote W. Thomas,[2]

"Properly speaking taboo includes only a) the sacred (or unclean) character of persons or

[1] Volkerpsychologie, II Band, "Mythus und Religion," 1906, II p. 308.

[2] Eleventh Edition, this article also gives the most important references.

things, b) the kind of prohibition which results
from this character, and c) the sanctity (or un-
cleanliness) which results from a violation of the
prohibition. The converse of taboo in Polynesia
is 'noa' and allied forms which mean 'general' or
'common' . . .

"Various classes of taboo in the wider sense
may be distinguished: 1. natural or direct, the
result of 'mana' (mysterious power) inherent in
a person or thing; 2. communicated or indirect,
equally the result of 'mana' but (a) acquired or
(b) imposed by a priest, chief or other person;
3. intermediate, where both factors are present,
as in the appropriation of a wife to her husband.
The term taboo is also applied to ritual prohibitions of a different nature; but its use in these
senses is better avoided. It might be argued
that the term should be extended to embrace
cases in which the sanction of the prohibition is
the creation of a god or spirit, i.e., to religious
interdictions as distinguished from magical, but
there is neither automatic action nor contagion
in such a case, and a better term for it is religious
interdiction.

"The objects of taboo are many: 1. direct
taboos aim at (a) protection of important persons—chiefs, priests, etc.—and things against
harm; (b) safeguarding of the weak—women,
children and common people generally—from the

powerful mana (magical influence) of chiefs and priests; (c) providing against the dangers incurred by handling or coming in contact with corpses, by eating certain food, etc.; (d) guarding the chief acts of life—births, initiation, marriage and sexual functions—against interference; (e) securing human beings against the wrath or power of gods and spirits; [3] (f) securing unborn infants and young children, who stand in a specially sympathetic relation with their parents, from the consequence of certain actions, and more especially from the communication of qualities supposed to be derived from certain foods. 2. Taboos are imposed in order to secure against thieves the property of an individual, his fields, tools, etc."

Other parts of the article may be summarized as follows. Originally the punishment for the violation of a taboo was probably left to an inner, automatic arrangement. The violated taboo avenged itself. Wherever the taboo was related to ideas of gods and demons an automatic punishment was expected from the power of the godhead. In other cases, probably as a result of a further development of the idea, society took over the punishment of the offender, whose action has endangered his companions.

[3] This application of the taboo can be omitted as not originally belonging in this connection.

Thus man's first systems of punishment are also connected with taboo.

"The violation of a taboo makes the offender himself taboo." The author goes on to say that certain dangers resulting from the violation of a taboo may be exercised through acts of penance and ceremonies of purification.

A peculiar power inherent in persons and ghosts, which can be transmitted from them to inanimate objects is regarded as the source of the taboo. This part of the article reads as follows: "Persons or things which are regarded as taboo may be compared to objects charged with electricity; they are the seat of tremendous power which is transmissible by contact, and may be liberated with destructive effect if the organisms which provoke its discharge are too weak to resist it; the result of a violation of a taboo depends partly on the strength of the magical influence inherent in the taboo object or person, partly on the strength of the opposing mana of the violator of the taboo. Thus, kings and chiefs are possessed of great power, and it is death for their subjects to address them directly; but a minister or other person of greater *mana* than common, can approach them unharmed, and can in turn be approached by their inferiors without risk. . . . So, too, indirect taboos depend for their strength on the mana of him who opposes them; if it is a chief or a priest, they are more powerful than those imposed by a common person."

The fact that a taboo is transmissible has surely given rise to the effort of removing it through expiatory ceremonies.

The author states that there are permanent and temporary taboos. The former comprise priest and chiefs as well as the dead and everything that has belonged to them. Temporary taboos attach themselves to certain conditions such as menstruation and child-bed, the status of the warrior before and after the expedition, the activities of fishing and of the chase, and similar activities. A general taboo may also be imposed upon a large district like an ecclesiastical interdict, and may then last for years.

If I judge my readers' impressions correctly I dare say that after hearing all that was said about taboo they are far from knowing what to understand by it and where to store it in their minds. This is surely due to the insufficient information I have given and to the omission of all discussions concerning the relation of taboo to superstition, to belief in the soul, and to religion. On the other hand, I fear that a more detailed description of what is known about taboo would be still more confusing; I can therefore assure the reader that the state of affairs is really

far from clear. We may say, however, that we
deal with a series of restrictions which these
primitive races impose upon themselves; this and
that is forbidden without any apparent reason;
nor does it occur to them to question this matter,
for they subject themselves to these restrictions
as a matter of course and are convinced that any
transgression will be punished automatically in
the most severe manner. There are reliable reports that innocent transgressions of such prohibitions have actually been punished automatically. For instance, the innocent offender who
had eaten from a forbidden animal became deeply
depressed, expected his death and then actually
died. The prohibitions mostly concern matters
which are capable of enjoyment such as freedom
of movement and unrestrained intercourse; in
some cases they appear very ingenious, evidently
representing abstinences and renunciations; in
other cases their content is quite incomprehensible, they seem to concern themselves with trifles
and give the impression of ceremonials. Something like a theory seems to underlie all these
prohibitions, it seems as if these prohibitions are
necessary because some persons and objects
possess a dangerous power which is transmitted
by contact with the object so charged, almost like
a contagion. The quantity of this dangerous
property is also taken into consideration. Some

persons or things have more of it than others and the danger is precisely in accordance with the charge. The most peculiar part of it is that any one who has violated such a prohibition assumes the nature of the forbidden object as if he had absorbed the whole dangerous charge. This power is inherent in all persons who are more or less prominent, such as kings, priests and the newly born, in all exceptional physical states such as menstruation, puberty and birth, in everything sinister like illness and death and in everything connected with these conditions by virtue of contagion or dissemination.

However, the term "taboo" includes all persons localities, objects and temporary conditions which are carriers or sources of this mysterious attribute. The prohibition derived from this attribute is also designated as taboo, and lastly taboo, in the literal sense, includes everything that is sacred, above the ordinary, and at the same time dangerous, unclean and mysterious.

Both this word and the system corresponding to it express a fragment of psychic life which really is not comprehensible to us. And indeed it would seem that no understanding of it could be possible without entering into the study of the belief in spirits and demons which is so characteristic of these low grades of culture.

Now why should we take any interest at all in

the riddle of taboo? Not only, I think, because every psychological problem is well worth the effort of investigation for its own sake, but for other reasons as well. It may be surmised that the taboo of Polynesian savages is after all not so remote from us as we were at first inclined to believe; the moral and customary prohibitions which we ourselves obey may have some essential relation to this primitive taboo the explanation of which may in the end throw light upon the dark origin of our own "categorical imperative."

We are therefore inclined to listen with keen expectations when an investigator like W. Wundt gives his interpretation of taboo, especially as he promises to "go back to the very roots of the taboo concepts." [4]

Wundt states that the idea of taboo "includes all customs which express dread of particular objects connected with cultic ideas or of actions having reference to them." [5]

On another occasion he says: "In accordance with the general sense of the word we understand by taboo every prohibition laid down in customs or manners or in expressly formulated laws, not to touch an object or to take it for one's own use, or to make use of certain proscribed

4 Volkerpsychologie, Vol. II, Religion und Mythus, p. 300.
5 l. c. p. 237.

words. . . ." Accordingly there would not be a single race or stage of culture which had escaped the injurious effects of taboo.

Wundt then shows why he finds it more practical to study the nature of taboo in the primitive states of Australian savages rather than in the higher culture of the Polynesian races. In the case of the Australians he divides taboo prohibitions into three classes according as they concern animals, persons or other objects. The animal taboo, which consists essentially of the taboo against killing and eating, forms the nucleus of Totemism.[6] The taboo of the second class, which has human beings for its object, is of an essentially different nature. To begin with it is restricted to conditions which bring about an unusual situation in life for the person tabooed. Thus young men at the feast of initiation, women during menstruation and immediately after delivery, newly born children, the diseased and especially the dead, are all taboo. The constantly used property of any person, such as his clothes, tools and weapons, is permanently taboo for everybody else. In Australia the new name which a youth receives at his initiation into manhood becomes part of his most personal property, it is taboo and must be kept secret. The taboos of the third class, which apply to trees, plants,

6 Comp. Chapter I.

houses and localities, are more variable and seem
only to follow the rule that anything which for
any reason arouses dread or is mysterious, becomes subject to taboo.

Wundt himself has to acknowledge that the
changes which taboo undergoes in the richer culture of the Polynesians and in the Malayan
Archipelago are not very profound. The
greater social differentiation of these races manifests itself in the fact that chiefs, kings and
priests exercise an especially effective taboo and
are themselves exposed to the strongest taboo
compulsion.

But the real sources of taboo lie deeper than
in the interests of the privileged classes: "They
begin where the most primitive and at the same
time the most enduring human impulses have
their origin, namely, *in the fear of the effect of
demonic powers.*" [7] "The taboo, which originally was nothing more than the objectified fear
of the demonic power thought to be concealed
in the tabooed object, forbids the irritation of
this power and demands the placation of the
demon whenever the taboo has been knowingly or
unknowingly violated."

The taboo then gradually became an autonom-
ous power which has detached itself from demonism. It becomes the compulsion of custom and

[7] l. c. p. 307.

tradition and finally of the law. "But the commandment concealed behind taboo prohibitions
which differ materially according to place and
time, had originally the meaning:  Beware of
the wrath of the demons."

Wundt therefore teaches that taboo is the expression and evolution of the belief of primitive races in demonic powers, and that later
taboo has dissociated itself from this origin and
has remained a power simply because it was one
by virtue of a kind of a psychic persistence and
in this manner it became the root of our customs
and laws.   As little as one can object to the first
part of this statement I feel, however, that I am
only voicing the impression of many of my readers if I call Wundt's explanation disappointing.
Wundt's explanation is far from going back to
the sources of taboo concepts or to their deepest
roots.   For neither fear nor demons can be accepted in psychology as finalities defying any
further deduction.  It would be different if
demons really existed; but we know that, like
gods, they are only the product of the psychic
powers of man; they have been created from and
out of something.

Wundt also expresses a number of important
though not altogether clear opinions about the
double meaning of taboo.   According to him the
division between *sacred* and *unclean* does not yet

exist in the first primitive stages of taboo. For this reason these conceptions entirely lack the significance which they could only acquire later on when they came to be contrasted. The animal, person, or place on which there is a taboo is demonic, that is, not sacred and therefore not yet, in the later sense, unclean. The expression taboo is particularly suitable for this undifferentiated and intermediate meaning of the demonic, in the sense of something which may not be touched, since it emphasizes a characteristic which finally adheres both to what is sacred and to the unclean, namely, the dread of contact. But the fact that this important characteristic is permanently held in common points to the existence of an original agreement here between these two spheres which gave way to a differentiation only as the result of further conditions through which both finally developed into opposites.

The belief associated with the original taboo, according to which a demonic power concealed in the object avenges the touching of it or its forbidden use by bewitching the offender was still an entirely objectified fear. This had not yet separated into the two forms which it assumed at a more developed stage, namely, awe and aversion.

How did this separation come about? According to Wundt, this was done through the transference of taboo prohibitions from the sphere of demons to that of theistic conceptions. The antithesis of sacred and unclean coincides with the succession of two mythological stages the first of which did not entirely disappear when the second was reached but continued in a state of greatly lowered esteem which gradually turned into contempt.  It is a general law in mythology that a preceding stage, just because it has been overcome and pushed back by a higher stage, maintains itself next to it in a debased form so that the objects of its veneration become objects of aversion.[8]

Wundt's further elucidations refer to the relation of taboo to lustration and sacrifice.

## 2

He who approaches the problem of taboo from the field of psychoanalysis, which is concerned with the study of the unconscious part of the individual's psychic life, needs but a moment's reflection to realize that these phenomena are by no means foreign to him.  He knows people who have individually created such taboo prohibitions for themselves, which they follow as strictly as savages observe the taboos common to their tribe or society.  If he were not accustomed to

[8] l. c. p. 313.

call these individuals "compulsion neurotics" he
would find the term "taboo disease" quite appropriate for their malady. Psychoanalytic investigation has taught him the clinical etiology
and the essential part of the psychological
mechanism of this compulsion disease, so that
he cannot resist applying what he has learnt
there to explain corresponding manifestations in
folk psychology.

There is one warning to which we shall have to
give heed in making this attempt. The similarity between taboo and compulsion disease may
be purely superficial, holding good only for the
manifestations of both without extending into
their deeper characteristics. Nature loves to
use identical forms in the most widely different
biological connections, as, for instance, for coral
stems and plants and even for certain crystals
or for the formation of certain chemical precipi-
tates. It would certainly be both premature and
unprofitable to base conclusions relating to inner relationships upon the correspondence of
merely mechanical conditions. We shall bear
this warning in mind without, however, giving up
our intended comparison on account of the possibility of such confusions.

The first and most striking correspondence between the compulsion prohibitions of neurotics
and taboo lies in the fact that the origin of these

prohibitions is just as unmotivated and enigmatic. They have appeared at some time or other and must now be retained on account of an unconquerable anxiety. An external threat of punishment is superfluous, because an inner certainty (a conscience) exists that violation will be followed by unbearable disaster. The very most that compulsion patients can tell us is the vague premonition that some person of their environment will suffer harm if they should violate the prohibition. Of what the harm is to consist is not known, and this inadequate information is more likely to be obtained during the later discussions of the expiatory and defensive actions than when the prohibitions themselves are being discussed.

As in the case of taboo the nucleus of the neurotic prohibition is the act of touching, whence we derive the name touching phobia, or *délire de toucher*. The prohibition extends not only to direct contact with the body but also to the figurative use of the phrase as "to come into contact," or "be in touch with some one or something." Anything that leads the thoughts to what is prohibited and thus calls forth mental contact is just as much prohibited as immediate bodily contact; this same extension is also found in taboo.

Some prohibitions are easily understood from

their purpose but others strike us as incomprehensible, foolish and senseless. We designate such commands as "ceremonials" and we find that taboo customs show the same variations.

Obsessive prohibitions possess an extraordinary capacity for displacement; they make use of almost any form of connection to extend from one object to another and then in turn make this new object "impossible," as one of my patients aptly puts it. This impossibility finally lays an embargo upon the whole world. The compulsion neurotics act as if the "impossible" persons and things were the carriers of a dangerous contagion which is ready to displace itself through contact to all neighboring things. We have already emphasized the same characteristics of contagion and transference in the description of taboo prohibitions. We also know that any one who has violated a taboo by touching something which is taboo becomes taboo himself, and no one may come into contact with him.

I shall put side by side two examples of transference or, to use a better term, displacement, one from the life of the Maori, and the other from my observation of a woman suffering from a compulsion neurosis:

"For a similar reason a Maori chief would not blow on a fire with his mouth; for his sacred breath would communicate its sanctity to the fire, which would pass it on to the meat in the pot, which would pass it on to the man who ate the meat, which was in the pot, which stood on the fire, which was breathed on by the chief; so that the eater, infected by the chief's breath conveyed through these intermediaries, would surely die." [9]

My patient demanded that a utensil which her husband had purchased and brought home should be removed lest it make the place where she lives impossible. For she has heard that this object was bought in a store which is situated, let us say, in Stag Street. But as the word stag is the name of a friend now in a distant city, whom she has known in her youth under her maiden name and whom she now finds "impossible," that is taboo, the object bought in Vienna is just as taboo as this friend with whom she does not want to come into contact.

Compulsion prohibitions, like taboo prohibitions, entail the most extraordinary renunciations and restrictions of life, but a part of these can be removed by carrying out certain acts which now also must be done because they have acquired a compulsive character (obsessive acts); there is no doubt that these acts are in the nature of penances, expiations, defense reactions, and puri-

[9] Frazer, "The Golden Bough," II, "Taboo and the Perils of the Soul," 1911, p. 136.

fications. The most common of these obsessive
acts is washing with water (washing obsession).
A part of the taboo prohibitions can also be replaced in this way, that is to say, their violation
can be made good through such a "ceremonial,"
and here too lustration through water is the preferred way.

Let us now summarize the points in which the
correspondence between taboo customs and the
symptoms of compulsion neurosis are most
clearly manifested: 1. In the lack of motivation of the commandments, 2. in their enforce-
ment through an inner need, 3. in their capacity
of displacement and in the danger of contagion
from what is prohibited, 4. and in the causation
of ceremonial actions and commandments which
emanate from the forbidden.

However, psychoanalysis has made us familiar
with the clinical history as well as the psychic
mechanism of compulsion neurosis. Thus the
history of a typical case of touching phobiá reads
as follows: In the very beginning, during the
early period of childhood, the person manifested
a strong pleasure in touching himself, the object
of which was much more specialized than one
would be inclined to expect. Presently the
carrying out of this very pleasurable act of
touching was opposed by a prohibition from

without.[10]   The prohibition was accepted because it was supported by strong inner forces; [11]
it proved to be stronger than the impulse which
wanted to manifest itself through this act of
touching.   But due to the primitive psychic constitution of the child this prohibition did not succeed in abolishing the impulse.   Its only success lay in repressing the impulse (the pleasure of
touching) and banishing it into the unconscious.
Both the prohibition and the impulse remained;
the impulse because it had only been repressed
and not abolished, the prohibition, because if it
had ceased the impulse would have broken
through into consciousness and would have been
carried out. . An unsolved situation, a psychic
fixation, had thus been created and now everything else emanated from the continued conflict
between prohibition and impulse.

The main characteristic of the psychic con-
stellation which has thus undergone fixation lies
in what one might call the ambivalent behavior [12]
of the individual to the object, or rather to an
action regarding it.   The individual constantly
wants to carry out this action (the act of touching), he sees in it the highest pleasure, but he

10 Both the pleasure and the prohibition referred to touching
one's own genitals.
11 The relation to beloved persons who impose the prohibition.
12 To use an excellent term coined by Bleuler.

may not carry it out, and he even abominates it. The opposition between these two streams cannot be easily adjusted because—there is no other way to express it—they are so localized in the psychic life that they cannot meet. The prohibition becomes fully conscious, while the surviving pleasure of touching remains unconscious, the person knowing nothing about it. If this psychological factor did not exist the ambivalence could neither maintain itself so long nor lead to such subsequent manifestations.

In the clinical history of the case we have emphasized the appearance of the prohibition in early childhood as the determining factor; but for the further elaboration of the neurosis this rôle is played by the repression which appears at this age. On account of the repression which has taken place, which is connected with forgetting (amnesia), the motivation of the prohibition that has become conscious remains unknown, and all attempts to unravel it intellectually must fail, as the point of attack cannot be found. The prohibition owes its strength—its compulsive character—to its association with its unknown counterpart, the hidden and unabated pleasure, that is to say, to an inner need into which conscious insight is lacking. The transferability and reproductive power of the prohibition reflect a process which harmonizes with the unconscious pleasure and is very much facilitated through the psychological determinants of the unconscious. The pleasure of the impulse constantly undergoes displacement in order to escape the blocking which it encounters and seeks to acquire surrogates for the forbidden in the form of substitutive objects and actions. For the same reason the prohibition also wanders and spreads to the new aims of the proscribed impulse. Every new advance of the repressed libido is answered by the prohibition with a new severity. The mutual inhibition of these two contending forces creates a need for discharge and for lessening the existing tension, in which we may recognize the motivation for the compulsive acts. In the neurosis there are distinctly acts of compromise which on the one hand may be regarded as proofs of remorse and efforts to expiate and similar actions; but on the other hand they are at the same time substitutive actions which recompense the impulse for what has been forbidden. It is a law of neurotic diseases that these obsessive acts serve the impulse more and more and come nearer and nearer to the original forbidden act.

We may now make the attempt to study taboo as if it were of the same nature as the compulsive prohibitions of our patients. It must naturally be clearly understood that many of the taboo prohibitions which we shall study are already second-

ary, displaced and distorted, so that we shall have
to be satisfied if we can shed some light upon the
earliest and most important taboo prohibitions.
We must also remember that the differences in
the situation of the savage and of the neurotic
may be important enough to exclude complete
correspondence and prevent a point by point
transfer from one to the other such as would be
possible if we were dealing with exact copies.

First of all it must be said that it is useless to
question savages as to the real motivation of their
prohibitions or as to the genesis of taboo. According to our assumption they must be incapable
of telling us anything about it since this motivation is "unconscious" to them. But following the
model of the compulsive prohibition we shall construct the history of taboo as follows: Taboos
are very ancient prohibitions which at one time
were forced upon a generation of primitive
people from without, that is, they probably were
forcibly impressed upon them by an earlier generation. These prohibitions concerned actions
for which there existed a strong desire. The prohibitions maintained themselves from generation
to generation, perhaps only as the result of a tradition set up by paternal and social authority.
But in later generations they have perhaps already become "organized" as a piece of inherited
psychic property. Whether there are such

"innate ideas" or whether these have brought about the fixation of the taboo by themselves or by coöperating with education no one could decide in the particular case in question. The persistence of taboo teaches, however, one thing, namely, that the original pleasure to do the forbidden still continues among taboo races. They therefore assume an *ambivalent attitude* toward their taboo prohibitions; in their unconscious they would like nothing better than to transgress them but they are also afraid to do it; they are afraid just because they would like to transgress, and the fear is stronger than the pleasure. But in every individual of the race the desire for it is unconscious, just as in the neurotic.

The oldest and most important taboo prohibitions are the two basic laws of *totemism:* namely not to kill the totem animal and to avoid sexual intercourse with totem companions of the other sex.

It would therefore seem that these must have been the oldest and strongest desires of mankind. We cannot understand this and therefore we cannot use these examples to test our assumptions as long as the meaning and the origin of the totemic system is so wholly unknown to us. But the very wording of these taboos and the fact that they occur together will remind any one who knows the results of the psychoanalytic investigation of individuals, of something quite definite which psychoanalysts call the central point of the infantile wish life and the nucleus of the later neurosis.[13]

All other varieties of taboo phenomena which have led to the attempted classifications noted above become unified if we sum them up in the following sentence:   The basis of taboo is a forbidden action for which there exists a strong inclination in the unconscious.

We know, without understanding it, that whoever does what is prohibited and violates the taboo, becomes himself taboo.   But how can we connect this fact with the other, namely that the taboo adheres not only to persons who have done what is prohibited but also to persons who are in exceptional circumstances, to these circumstances themselves, and to impersonal things?   What can this dangerous attribute be, which always remains the same under all these different conditions?   Only one thing, namely, the propensity to arouse the ambivalence of man and to tempt him to violate the prohibition.

An individual who has violated a taboo becomes himself taboo because he has the dangerous property of tempting others to follow his example. He arouses envy; why should he be allowed to do what is prohibited to others?   He is therefore really *contagious*, in so far as every example in-

[13] See Chapter IV Totemism, etc.

cites to imitation, and therefore he himself must be avoided.

But a person may become permanently or temporarily taboo without having violated any taboos, for the simple reason that he is in a condition which has the property of inciting the forbidden desires of others and of awakening the ambivalent conflict in them. Most of the exceptional positions and conditions have this charácter and possess this dangerous power. The king or chieftain rouses envy of his prerogatives; everybody would perhaps like to be king. The dead, the newly born, and women when they are incapacitated, all act as incitements on account of their peculiar helplessness, while the individual who has just reached sexual maturity tempts through the promise of a new pleasure. Therefore all these persons and all these conditions are taboo, for one must not yield to the temptations which they offer.

Now, too, we understand why the forces inherent in the "mana" of various persons can neutralize one another so that the mana of one individual can partly cancel that of the other. The taboo of a king is too strong for his subject because the social difference between them is too great. But a minister, for example, can become the harmless mediator between them. Translated from the language of taboo into the language of normal psychology this means: the subject who shrinks from the tremendous temptation which contact with the king creates for him can brook the intercourse of an official, whom he does not have to envy so much and whose position perhaps seems attainable to him. The minister, on his part, can moderate his envy of the king by taking into consideration the power that has been granted to him. Thus smaller differences in the magic power that lead to temptation are less to be feared than exceptionally big differences.

It is equally clear how the violation of certain taboo prohibitions becomes a social danger which must be punished or expiated by all the members of society lest it harm them all. This danger really exists if we substitute the known impulses for the unconscious desires. It consists in the possibility of imitation, as a result of which society would soon be dissolved. If the others did not punish the violation they would perforce become aware that they want to imitate the evil doer.

Though the secret meaning of a taboo prohibition cannot possibly be of so special a nature as in the case of a neurosis, we must not be astonished to find that touching plays a similar rôle in taboo prohibition as in the *délire de toucher*. To touch is the beginning of every act of possession, of every attempt to make use of a person or thing.

We have interpreted the power of contagion which inheres in the taboo as the property of leading into temptation, and of inciting to imitation. This does not seem to be in accord with the fact that the contagiousness of the taboo is above all manifested in the transference to objects which thus themselves become carriers of the taboo.

This transferability of the taboo reflects what is found in the neurosis, namely, the constant tendency of the unconscious impulse to become displaced through associative channels upon new objects.    Our attention is thus drawn to the fact that the dangerous magic power of the "mana" corresponds to two real faculties, the capacity of reminding man of his forbidden wishes, and the apparently more important one of tempting him to violate the prohibition in the service of these wishes.    Both functions reunite into one, however, if we assume it to be in accord with a primitive psychic life that with the awakening of a memory of a forbidden action there should also be combined the awakening of the tendency to carry out the action.    Memory and temptation then again coincide.    We must also admit that if the example of a person who has violated a prohibition leads another to the same action, the disobedience of the prohibition has been transmitted like a contagion, just as the taboo is transferred from a person to an object, and from this to another.

If the violation of a taboo can be condoned through expiation or penance, which means, of course, a *renunciation* of a possession or a liberty, we have the proof that the observance of a taboo regulation was itself a renunciation of something really wished for. The omission of one renunciation is cancelled through a renunciation at some other point. This would lead us to conclude that, as far as taboo ceremonials are concerned, penance is more primitive than purification.

Let us now summarize what understanding we have gained of taboo through its comparison with the compulsive prohibition of the neurotic. Taboo is a very primitive prohibition imposed from without (by an authority) and directed against the strongest desires of man. The desire to violate it continues in the unconscious; persons who obey the taboo have an ambivalent feeling toward what is affected by the taboo. The magic power attributed to taboo goes back to its ability to lead man into temptation; it behaves like a contagion, because the example is contagious, and because the prohibited desire becomes displacing in the unconscious upon something else. The expiation for the violation of a taboo through a renunciation proves that a renunciation is at the basis of the observance of the taboo.

### 3

We may ask what we have gained from the comparison of taboo with compulsion neurosis and what value can be claimed for the interpretation we have given on the basis of this comparison? Our interpretation is evidently of no value unless it offers an advantage not to be had in any other way and unless it affords a better understanding of taboo than was otherwise possible. We might claim that we have already given proof of its usefulness in what has been said above; but we shall have to try to strengthen our proof by continuing the explanation of taboo prohibitions and customs in detail.

But we can avail ourselves of another method. We can shape our investigation so as to ascertain whether a part of the assumptions which we have transferred from the neurosis to the taboo, or the conclusions at which we have thereby arrived can be demonstrated directly in the phenomena of taboo. We must decide, however, what we want to look for. The assertion concerning the genesis of taboo, namely, that it was derived from a primitive prohibition which was once imposed from without, cannot, of course, be proved. We shall therefore seek to confirm those psychological conditions for taboo with which we have become acquainted in the case of compulsion neurosis. How did we gain our knowledge of these psychological factors in the case of neurosis? Through the analytical study of the symptoms, especially the compulsive actions, the defense reactions and the obsessive commands. These mechanisms gave every indication of having been derived from *ambivalent* impulses or tendencies, they either represented simultaneously the wish and counter-wish or they served preponderantly one of the two contrary tendencies. If we should now succeed in showing that ambivalence, i. e., the sway of contrary tendencies, exists also in the case of taboo regulations or if we should find among the taboo mechanisms some which like neurotic obsessions give simultaneous expression to both currents, we would have established what is practically the most important point in the psychological correspondence between taboo and compulsion neurosis.

We have already mentioned that the two fundamental taboo prohibitions are inaccessible to our analysis because they belong to totemism; another part of the taboo rules is of secondary origin and cannot be used for our purpose. For among these races taboo has become the general form of law giving and has helped to promote social tendencies which are certainly younger than taboo itself, as for instance, the taboos imposed by chiefs and priests to insure their property and privileges. But there still remains a large group of laws which we may undertake to investigate. Among these I lay stress on those taboos which are attached a) to enemies, b) to chiefs, and c) to the dead; the material for our investigation is taken from the excellent collection of J. G. Frazer in his great work, "The Golden Bough." [14]

## A) THE TREATMENT OF ENEMIES

Inclined as we may have been to ascribe to savage and semi-savage races uninhibited and remorseless cruelty towards their enemies, it is of great interest to us to learn that with them, too, the killing of a person compels the observation of a series of rules which are associated with taboo customs. These rules are easily brought under four groups; they demand 1. reconciliation with the slain enemy, 2. restrictions, 3. acts of expiation, and purifications of the manslayer, and 4. certain ceremonial rites. The incomplete reports do not allow us to decide with certainty how general or how isolated such taboo customs may be

[14] Third Edition, Part II, "Taboo and the Perils of the Soul," 1911.

among these races, but this is a matter of indifference as far as our interest in these occurrences is concerned. Still, it may be assumed that we are dealing with widespread customs and not with isolated peculiarities.

The reconciliation customs practiced on the island of Timor, after a victorious band of warriors has returned with the severed heads of the vanquished enemy, are especially significant because the leader of the expedition is subject to heavy additional restrictions. "At the solemn entry of the victors, sacrifices are made to conciliate the souls of the enemy; otherwise one would have to expect harm to come to the victors. A dance is given and a song is sung in which the slain enemy is mourned and his forgiveness is implored: 'Be not angry,' they say, 'because your head is here with us; had we been less lucky, our heads might have been exposed in your village. We have offered the sacrifice to appease you. Your spirit may now rest and leave us at peace. Why were you our enemy? Would it not have been better that we should remain friends? Then your blood would not have been spilt and your head would not have been cut off.' " [15]

Similar customs are found among the Palu in Celebes; the Gallas sacrifice to the spirits of their

[15] Frazer, l. c. p. 166.

dead enemies before they return to their home villages.[16]

Other races have found methods of making friends, guardians and protectors out of their former enemies after they are dead. This consists in the tender treatment of the severed heads, of which many wild tribes of Borneo boast. When the See-Dayaks of Sarawak bring home a head from a war expedition, they treat it for months with the greatest kindness and courtesy and address it with the most endearing names in their language. The best morsels from their meals are put into its mouth, together with titbits and cigars. The dead enemy is repeatedly entreated to hate his former friends and to bestow his love upon his new hosts because he has now become one of them. It would be a great mistake to think that any derision is attached to this treatment, horrible though it may seem to us.[17]

Observers have been struck by the mourning for the enemy after he is slain and scalped, among several of the wild tribes of North America. When a Choctaw had killed an enemy he began a month's mourning during which he submitted himself to serious restrictions. The Dakota Indians mourned in the same way. One authority

[16] Paulitschke, "Ethnography of Northeast Africa."
[17] Frazer, "Adonis, Attis, Osiris," p. 248, 1907. According to Hugh Low, Sarawak, London, 1848.

mentions that the Osaga Indians after mourning
for their own dead mourned for their foes as if
they had been friends.[18]

Before proceeding to the other classes of taboo
customs for the treatment of enemies, we must
define our position in regard to a pertinent objection. Both Frazer as well as other authorities
may well be quoted against us to show that the
motive for these rules of reconciliation is quite
simple and has nothing to do with "ambivalence."
These races are dominated by a superstitious fear
of the spirits of the slain, a fear which was also
familiar to classical antiquity, and which the
great British dramatist brought upon the stage
in the hallucinations of Macbeth and Richard the
Third. From this superstition all the reconciliation rules as well as the restrictions and expiations which we shall discuss later can be logically
deduced; moreover, the ceremonies included in
the fourth group also argue for this interpretation, since the only explanation of which they
admit is the effort to drive away the spirits of the
slain which pursue the manslayers.[19] Besides,
the savages themselves directly admit their fear
of the spirits of their slain foes and trace back
the taboo customs under discussion to this fear.

18 J. O. Dorsay, see Frazer, "Toboo, etc.," p. 181.
19 Frazer, "Taboo," p. 166 to 174. These ceremonies consist of
hitting shields, shouting, bellowing and making noises with various
instruments, etc.

This objection is certainly pertinent and if it were adequate as well we would gladly spare ourselves the trouble of our attempt to find a further explanation. We postpone the consideration of this objection until later and for the present merely contrast it to the interpretation derived from our previous discussion of taboo. All these rules of taboo lead us to conclude that other impulses besides those that are merely hostile find expression in the behavior towards enemies. We see in them manifestations of repentance, of regard for the enemy, and of a bad conscience for having slain him. It seems that the commandment, Thou shalt not slay, which could not be violated without punishment, existed also among these savages, long before any legislation was received from the hands of a god.

We now return to the remaining classes of taboo rules. The *restrictions* laid upon the victorious manslayer are unusually frequent and are mostly of a serious nature. In Timor (compare the reconciliation customs mentioned above) the leader of the expedition cannot return to his house under any circumstances. A special hut is erected for him in which he spends two months engaged in the observance of various rules of purification. During this period he may not see his wife or nourish himself; another person must

put his food into his mouth.[20] Among some
Dayak tribes warriors returning from a successful expedition must remain sequestered for several days and abstain from certain foods; they
may not touch iron and must remain away from
their wives. In Logea, an island near New
Guinea, men who have killed an enemy or have
taken part in the killing, lock themselves up in
their houses for a week. They avoid every intercourse with their wives and friends, they do not
touch their victuals with their hands and live on
nothing but vegetable foods which are cooked
for them in special dishes. As a reason for this
last restriction it is alleged that they must smell
the blood of the slain, otherwise they would sicken
and die. Among the Toaripi- or Motumotu-
tribes in New Guinea a manslayer must not approach his wife and must not touch his food with
his fingers. A second person must feed him with
special food. This continues until the next new
moon.

I avoid the complete enumeration of all the
cases of restrictions of the victorious slayer mentioned by Frazer, and emphasize only such cases
in which the character of taboo is especially noticeable or where the restriction appears in con-

[20] Frazer, "Taboo," p. 166, according to S. Mueller, "Reisen en
Onderzoekingen in den Indischen Archipel," Amsterdam, 1857.

nection with expiation, purification and ceremonial.

Among the Monumbos in German New
Guinea a man who has killed an enemy in combat
becomes "unclean," the same word being employed which is applied to women during menstruation or confinement. For a considerable
period he is not allowed to leave the men's clubhouse, while the inhabitants of his village gather
about him and celebrate his victory with songs
and dances. He must not touch any one, not
even his wife and children; if he did so they would
be afflicted with boils. He finally becomes clean
through washing and other ceremonies.

Among the Natchez in North America young
warriors who had procured their first scalp were
bound for six months to the observance of certain
renunciations. They were not allowed to sleep
with their wives or to eat meat, and received only
fish and maize pudding as nourishment. When a
Choctaw had killed and scalped an enemy he
began a period of mourning for one month, during which he was not allowed to comb his hair.
When his head itched he was not allowed to
scratch it with his hand but used a small stick for
this purpose.

After a Pima Indian had killed an Apache he
had to submit himself to severe ceremonies of

purification and expiation. During a fasting period of sixteen days he was not allowed to touch meat or salt, to look at a fire or to speak to any one. He lived alone in the woods, where he was waited upon by an old woman who brought him a small allowance of food; he often bathed in the nearest river, and carried a lump of clay on his head as a sign of mourning. On the seventeenth day there took place a public ceremony through which he and his weapons were solemnly purified. As the Pima Indians took the manslayer taboo much more seriously than their enemies and, unlike them, did not postpone expiation and purification until the end of the expedition, their prowess in war suffered very much through their moral severity or what might be called their piety. In spite of their extraordinary bravery they proved to be unsatisfactory allies to the Americans in their wars against the Apaches.

The detail and variations of these expiatory and purifying ceremonies after the killing of an enemy would be most interesting for purposes of a more searching study but I need not enumerate any more of them here because they cannot furnish us with any new points of view. I might mention that the temporary or permanent isolation of the professional executioner, which was maintained up to our time, is a case in point. The position of the "free-holder" in mediæval society really conveys a good idea of the "taboo" of savages.[21]

The current explanation of all these rules of reconciliation, restriction, expiation and purification, combines two principles, namely, the extension of the taboo of the dead to everything that has come into contact with him, and the fear of the spirit of the slain.  In what combination these two elements are to explain the ceremonial, whether they are to be considered as of equal value or whether one of them is primary and the other secondary, and which one, is nowhere stated, nor would this be an easy matter to decide.  In contradistinction to all this we emphasize the unity which our interpretation gains by deducing all these rules from the ambivalence of the emotion of savages towards their enemies.

### B)   THE TABOO OF RULERS

The behavior of primitive races towards their chiefs, kings, and priests, is controlled by two principles which seem rather to supplement than to contradict each other.  They must both be guarded and be guarded against.[22]

Both objects are accomplished through innumerable rules of taboo.  Why one must guard

---

21 For these examples see Frazer, "Taboo," p. 165–170, "Manslayers Tabooed."

22 Frazer, "Taboo," p. 132.  "He must not only be guarded, he must also be guarded against."

against rulers is already known to us; because
they are the bearers of that mysterious and dangerous magic power which communicates itself
by contact, like an electric charge, bringing death
and destruction to any one not protected by a
similar charge. All direct or indirect contact
with this dangerous sacredness is therefore
avoided, and where it cannot be avoided a ceremonial has been found to ward off the dreaded
consequences. The Nubas in East Africa, for
instance, believe that they must die if they enter
the house of their priest-king, but that they
escape this danger if, on entering, they bare the
left shoulder and induce the king to touch it with
his hand. Thus we have the remarkable case of
the king's touch becoming the healing and protective measure against the very dangers that arise
from contact with the king; but it is probably a
question of the healing power of the intentional
touching on the king's part in contradistinction
to the danger of touching him, in other words, of
the opposition between passivity and activity
towards the king.

Where the healing power of the royal touch is
concerned we do not have to look for examples
among savages. In comparatively recent times
the kings of England exercised this power upon
scrofula, whence it was called "The King's Evil."
Neither Queen Elizabeth nor any of her suc-

cessors renounced this part of the royal prerogative.    Charles I is said to have healed a hundred
sufferers at one time, in the year 1633.    Under
his dissolute son Charles II, after the great
English revolution had passed, royal healings of
scrofula attained their greatest vogue.

This king is said to have touched close to a
hundred thousand victims of scrofula in the
course of his reign.    The crush of those seeking
to be cured used to be so great that on one occasion six or seven patients suffered death by suffo-
cation instead of being healed.    The skeptical
king of Orange, William III, who became king
of England after the banishment of the Stuarts,
refused to exercise the spell; on the one occasion
when he consented to practice the touch, he did
so with the words:    "May God give you better
health and more sense." [23]

The following account will bear witness to the
terrible effect of touching by virtue of which a
person, even though unintentionally, becomes
active against his king or against what belongs to
him.    A chief of high rank and great holiness in
New Zealand happened to leave the remains of
his meal by the roadside.    A young slave came
along, a strong, healthy fellow, who saw what
was left over and started to eat it.    Hardly had
he finished when a horrified spectator informed

[23] Frazer, The Magic Art I, p. 368.

him of his offense in eating the meal of the chief.
The man had been a strong, brave, warrior, but
as soon as he heard this he collapsed and was
afflicted by terrible convulsions, from which he
died towards sunset of the following day.[24] A
Maori woman ate a certain fruit and then learned
that it came from a place on which there was a
taboo. She cried out that the spirit of the chief
whom she had thus offended would surely kill
her. This incident occurred in the afternoon and
on the next day at twelve o'clock she was dead.[25]
The tinder box of a Maori chief once cost several
persons their lives. The chief had lost it and
those who found it used it to light their pipes.
When they learned whose property the tinder
box was they all died of fright.[26]

It is hardly astonishing that the need was felt
to isolate dangerous persons like chiefs and
priests, by building a wall around them which
made them inaccessible to others. We surmise
that this wall, which originally was constructed
out of taboo rules, still exists to-day in the form
of court ceremony.

But probably the greater part of this taboo of
the rulers cannot be traced back to the need of

[24] "Old New Zealand," by a Pakeha Maori (London, 1884), see
Frazer, "Taboo," p. 135.
[25] W. Brown, "New Zealand and Its Aborigines" (London,
1845), Frazer, ibid.
[26] Frazer, l. c.

guarding against them. The other point of view
in the treatment of privileged persons, the need
of guarding them from dangers with which they
are threatened, has had a distinct share in the
creation of taboo and therefore of the origin of
court etiquette.

The necessity of guarding the king from every
conceivable danger arises from his great importance for the weal and woe of his subjects.
Strictly speaking, he is a person who regulates
the course of the world; his people have to thank
him not only for rain and sunshine, which allow
the fruits of the earth to grow, but also for the
wind which brings the ships to their shores and for
the solid ground on which they set their feet.[27]

These savage kings are endowed with a wealth
of power and an ability to bestow happiness
which only gods possess; certainly in later
stages of civilization none but the most servile
courtiers would play the hypocrite to the extent
of crediting their sovereigns with the possession
of attributes similar to these.

It seems like an obvious contradiction that persons of such perfection of power should themselves require the greatest care to guard them
against threatening dangers, but this is not the
only contradiction revealed in the treatment of
royal persons on the part of savages. These

[27] Frazer, "Taboo." "The Burden of Royalty," p. 7.

races consider it necessary to watch over their
kings to see that they use their powers in the right
way; they are by no means sure of their good intentions or of their conscientiousness. A strain
of mistrust is mingled with the motivation of the
taboo rules for the king. "The idea that early
kingdoms are despotisms," says Frazer,[28] "in
which the people exist only for the sovereign, is
wholly inapplicable to the monarchies we are con-
sidering. On the contrary, the sovereign in them
exists only for his subjects; his life is only valuable so long as he discharges the duties of his
position by ordering the course of nature for his
people's benefit. So soon as he fails to do so,
the care, the devotion, the religious homage which
they had hitherto lavished on him cease and are
changed into hatred and contempt; he is igno-
miniously dismissed and may be thankful if he
escapes with his life. Worshiped as a god one
day, he is killed as a criminal the next. But in
this changed behavior of the people there is nothing capricious or inconsistent. On the contrary,
their conduct is quite consistent. If their king
is their god he is, or should be, also their pre-
server; and if he will not preserve them he must
make room for another who will. So long, however, as he answers their expectations, there is no
limit to the care which they take of him, and which

28 l. c., p. 7.

they compel him to take of himself.   A king of
this sort lives hedged in by ceremonious etiquette,
a network of prohibitions and observances, of
which the intention is not to contribute to his dignity, much less to his comfort, but to restrain him
from conduct which, by disturbing the harmony
of nature, might involve himself, his people, and
the universe in one common catastrophe.   Far
from adding to his comfort, these observances,
by trammeling his every act, annihilate his freedom and often render the very life, which it is
their object to preserve, a burden and sorrow to
him."

One of the most glaring examples of thus fet-
tering and paralyzing a holy ruler through taboo
ceremonial seems to have been reached in the life
routine of the Mikado of Japan, as it existed in
earlier centuries.   A description which is now over
two hundred years old [29] relates:   "He thinks
that it would be very prejudicial to his dignity
and holiness to touch the ground with his feet;
for this reason when he intends to go anywhere,
he must be carried thither on men's shoulders.
Much less will they suffer that he should expose
his sacred person to the open air, and the sun is
not thought worthy to shine on his head.   There
is such a holiness ascribed to all the parts of his
body that he dares to cut off neither his hair,

29 Kaempfer, "History of Japan," see in Frazer, l. c., p. 3.

nor his beard, nor his nails. However, lest he
should grow too dirty, they may clean him in the
night when he is asleep; because they say that
what is taken from his body at that time, hath
been stolen from him, and that such a theft does
not prejudice his holiness or dignity. In ancient
times, he was obliged to sit on the throne for some
hours every morning, with the imperial crown on
his head; but to sit altogether like a statue without stirring either hands or feet, head or eyes, nor
indeed any part of his body, because by this
means, it was thought that he could preserve
peace and tranquility in his empire; for if unfortunately, he turned himself on one side or
other, or if he looked a good while towards any
part of his dominion, it was apprehended that
war, famine, fire or some other great misfortune
was near at hand to desolate the country."

Some of the taboos to which barbarian kings
are subject vividly recall the restrictions placed
on murderers. On Shark Point at Cape Padron
in Lower Guinea (West Africa), a priest-king
called Kukulu lives alone in a woods. He is not
allowed to touch a woman or to leave his house
and cannot even rise out of his chair, in which he
must sleep in a sitting position. If he should lie
down the wind would cease and shipping would
be disturbed. It is his function to keep storms in
check and, in general, to see to an even, healthy

condition of the atmosphere.[30]    The more powerful a king of Loango is, says Bastian, the more
taboos he must observe.    The heir to the throne
is also bound to them from childhood on; they
accumulate about him while he is growing up, and
by the time of his accession he is suffocated by
them.

Our interest in the matter does not require us
to take up more space to describe more fully the
taboos that cling to royal and priestly dignity.
We merely add that restrictions as to freedom of
movement and diet play the main rôle among
them.    But two examples of taboo ceremonial
taken from civilized nations, and therefore from
much higher stages of culture, will indicate to
what an extent association with these privileged
persons tends to preserve ancient customs.

The Flamen *Dialis,* the high-priest of Jupiter
in Rome, had to observe an extraordinarily large
number of taboo rules.    He was not allowed to
ride, to see a horse or an armed man, to wear a
ring that was not broken, to have a knot in his
garments, to touch wheat flour or leaven, or even
to mention by name a goat, a dog, raw meat,
beans and ivy; his hair could only be cut by a free
man and with a bronze knife, his hair combings
and nail parings had to be buried under a lucky

[30] Bastian, "The German Expedition to the Coast of Loango."
Jena 1874, cited by Frazer, l. c., p. 5.

tree; he could not touch the dead, go into the open with bare head, and similar prohibitions. His wife, the Flaminica, also had her own prohibitions: she was not allowed to ascend more than three steps on a certain kind of stairs and on certain holidays she could not comb her hair; the leather for her shoes could not be taken from any animal that had died a natural death but only from one that had been slaughtered or sacrificed; when she heard thunder she was unclean until she had made an expiatory sacrifice.[31]

The old kings of Ireland were subject to a series of very curious restrictions, the observance of which was expected to bring every blessing to the country while their violation entailed every form of evil. The complete description of these taboos is given in the Book of Rights, of which the oldest manuscript copies bear the dates 1390 and 1418. The prohibitions are very detailed and concern certain activities at specified places and times; in some cities, for instance, the king cannot stay on a certain day of the week, while at some specified hour this or that river may not be crossed, or again there is a plane on which he cannot camp a full nine days, etc.[32]

Among many savage races the severity of the taboo restrictions for the priest-kings has had results of historic importance which are especially

31 Frazer, l. c., p. 13.　　32 Frazer, l.c., p. 11.

interesting from our point of view. The honor
of being a priest-king ceased to be desirable; the
person in line for the succession often used every
means to escape it. Thus in Combodscha, where
there is a fire and water king, it is often necessary
to use force to compel the successor to accept the
honor. On Nine or Savage Island, a coral
island in the Pacific Ocean, monarchy actually
came to an end because nobody was willing to undertake the responsible and dangerous office. In
some parts of West Africa a general council is
held after the death of the king to determine upon
the successor. The man on whom the choice
falls is seized, tied and kept in custody in the
fetich house until he has declared himself willing
to accept the crown. Sometimes the presump-
tive successor to the throne finds ways and means
to avoid the intended honor; thus it is related of
a certain chief that he used to go armed day and
night and resist by force every attempt to place
him on the throne.[33] Among the negroes of
Sierra Leone the resistance against accepting the
kingly honor was so great that most of the tribes
were compelled to make strangers their kings.

Frazer makes these conditions responsible for
the fact that in the development of history a separation of the original priest-kingship into a spir-

[33] A. Bastian, "The German Expedition on the Coast of
Lonago," cited by Frazer, l. c., p. 18.

itual and a secular power finally took place.
Kings, crushed by the burden of their holiness,
became incapable of exercising their power over
real things and had to leave this to inferior but
executive persons who were willing to renounce
the honors of royal dignity. From these there
grew up the secular rulers, while the spiritual
over-lordship, which was now of no practical importance, was left to the former taboo kings. It
is well known to what extent this hypothesis finds
confirmation in the history of old Japan.

A survey of the picture of the relations of
primitive peoples to their rulers gives rise to the
expectation that our advance from description
to psychoanalytic understanding will not be
difficult. These relations are of an involved
nature and are not free from contradictions.
Rulers are granted great privileges which are
practically cancelled by taboo prohibitions in
regard to other privileges. They are privileged
persons, they can do or enjoy what is withheld
from the rest through taboo. But in contrast
to this freedom they are restricted by other taboos
which do not affect the ordinary individual.
Here, therefore, is the first contrast, which
amounts almost to a contradiction, between an
excess of freedom and an excess of restriction as
applied to the same persons. They are credited
with extraordinary magic powers and contact

with their person or their property is therefore feared, while on the other hand the most beneficial effect is expected from these contacts. This seems to be a second and an especially glaring contradiction; but we have already learned that it is only apparent.  The king's touch, exercised by him with benevolent intention, heals and protects; it is only when a common man touches the king or his royal effects that the contact becomes dangerous, and this is probably because the act may recall aggressive tendencies.  Another contradiction which is not so easily solved is expressed in the fact that great power over the processes of nature is ascribed to the ruler and yet the obligation is felt to guard him with especial care against threatening dangers, as if his own power, which can do so much, were incapable of accomplishing this.  A further difficulty in the relation arises because there is no confidence that the ruler will use his tremendous power to the advantage of his subjects as well as for his own protection; he is therefore distrusted and surveillance over him is considered to be justified.  The taboo etiquette, to which the life of the king is subject, simultaneously serves all these objects of exercising a tutelage over the king, of guarding him against dangers, and of guarding his subjects against danger which he brings to them.

We are inclined to give the following explanation of the complicated and contradictory relation of primitive peoples to their rulers.
Through superstition as well as through other
motives, various tendencies find expression in
the treatment of kings, each of which is developed to the extreme without regard to the others.
As a result of this, contradictions arise at which
the intellect of savages takes no more offense
than a highly civilized person would, as long as
it is only a question of religious matters or of
"loyalty."

That would be so far so good; but the psychoanalytic technique may enable us to penetrate
more deeply into the matter and to add something about the nature of these various tendencies. If we subject the facts as stated to analysis, just as if they formed the symptoms of a
neurosis, our first attention would be directed
to the excess of anxious worry which is said to be
the cause of the taboo ceremonial. The occurrence of such excessive tenderness is very common in the neurosis and especially in the
compulsion neurosis upon which we are drawing primarily for our comparison. We now
thoroughly understand the origin of this tenderness. It occurs wherever, besides the predominant tenderness, there exists a contrary but unconscious stream of hostility, that is to say, wher-

ever the typical case of an ambivalent affective attitude is realized. The hostility is then cried down by an excessive increase of tenderness which is expressed as anxiety and becomes compulsive because otherwise it would not suffice for its task of keeping the unconscious opposition in a state of repression. Every psychoanalyst knows how infallibly this anxious excess of tenderness can be resolved even under the most improbable circumstances, as for instance, when it appears between mother and child, or in the case of affectionate married people. Applied to the treatment of privileged persons this theory of an ambivalent feeling would reveal that their veneration, their very deification, is opposed in the unconscious by an intense hostile tendency, so that, as we had expected, the situation of an ambivalent feeling is here realized. The distrust which certainly seems to contribute to the motivation of the royal taboo, would be another direct manifestation of the same unconscious hostility. Indeed the ultimate issues of this conflict show such a diversity among different races that we would not be at a loss for examples in which the proof of such hostility would be much easier. We learn from Frazer [34] that the savage Timmes of Sierra Leona reserve the right to ad-

<hr />

[34] l. c. p. 18. According to Zwefel et Moustier, "Voyage aux Sources du Niger," 1880.

minister a beating to their elected king on the
evening before his coronation, and that they
make use of this constitutional right with such
thoroughness that the unhappy ruler sometimes
does not long survive his accession to the throne;
for this reason the leaders of the race have made
it a rule to elect some man against whom they
have a particular grudge. Nevertheless, even in
such glaring cases the hostility is not acknowledged as such, but is expressed as if it were a
ceremonial.

Another trait in the attitude of primitive races
towards their rulers recalls a mechanism which is
universally present in mental disturbances, and
is openly revealed in the so-called delusions of
persecution. Here the importance of a particular person is extraordinarily heightened and his
omnipotence is raised to the improbable in order
to make it easier to attribute to him the responsibility for everything painful which happens to
the patient. Savages really do not act differ-
ently towards their rulers when they ascribe to
them power over rain and shine, wind and
weather, and then dethrone or kill them because
nature has disappointed their expectation of a
good hunt or a ripe harvest. The prototype
which the paranoiac reconstructs in his persecution mania, is found in the relation of the child
to its father. Such omnipotence is regularly at-

tributed to the father in the imagination of the
son, and distrust of the father has been shown
to be intimately connected with the highest esteem for him.   When a paranoiac names a person of his acquaintance as his "persecutor," he
thereby elevates him to the paternal succession
and brings him under conditions which enable him
to make him responsible for all the misfortune
which he experiences.   Thus this second analogy
between the savage and the neurotic may allow
us to surmise how much in the relation of the savage to his ruler arises from the infantile attitude
of the child to its father.

But the strongest support for our point of
view, which seeks to compare taboo prohibitions
with neurotic symptoms, is to be found in the
taboo ceremonial itself, the significance of which
for the status of kinship has already been the subject of our previous discussion.   This ceremonial
unmistakably reveals its double meaning and its
origin from ambivalent tendencies if only we are
willing to assume that the effects it produces are
those which it intended from the very beginning.
It not only distinguishes kings and elevates them
above all ordinary mortals, but it also makes
their life a torture and an unbearable burden and
forces them into a thraldom which is far worse
than that of their subjects.   It would thus be
the correct counterpart to the compulsive ac-

tion of the neurosis, in which the suppressed impulse and the impulse which suppreses it meet in mutual and simultaneous satisfaction. The compulsive action is nominally a protection against the forbidden action; but we would say that actually it is a repetition of what is forbidden. The word "nominally" is here applied to the conscious whereas the word "actually" applies to the unconscious instance of the psychic life. Thus also the taboo ceremonial of kings is nominally an expression of the highest veneration and a means of guarding them; actually it is the punishment for their elevation, the revenge which their subjects take upon them. The experiences which Cervantes makes Sancho Panza undergo as governor on his island have evidently made him recognize this interpretation of courtly ceremonial as the only correct one. It is very possible that this point would be corroborated if we could induce kings and rulers of to-day to express themselves on this point.

Why the emotional attitude towards rulers should contain such a strong unconscious share of hostility is a very interesting problem which, however, exceeds the scope of this book. We have already referred to the infantile father-complex; we may add that an investigation of the early history of kingship would bring the decisive explanations. Frazer has an impressive discus-

sion of the theory that the first kings were
strangers who, after a short reign, were destined
to be sacrificed at solemn festivals as representatives of the deity; but Frazer himself does not
consider his facts altogether convincing.[35]
Christian myths are said to have been still influenced by the after-effects of this evolution of
kings.

### c) THE TABOO OF THE DEAD

We know that the dead are mighty rulers: we
may be surprised to learn that they are regarded
as enemies.

Among most primitive people the taboo of the
dead displays, if we may keep to our infection
analogy, a peculiar virulence. It manifests itself in the first place, in the consequences which
result from contact with the dead, and in the
treatment of the mourners for the dead. Among
the Maori any one who had touched a corpse or
who had taken part in its interment, became extremely unclean and was almost cut off from intercourse with his fellow beings; he was, as we
say, boycotted. He could not enter a house, or
approach persons or objects without infecting
them with the same properties. He could not
even touch his food with his own hands, which

[35] Frazer, "The Magic Act and the Evolution of Kings," 2 vols.,
1911. (The Golden Bough.)

were now unclean and therefore quite useless to
him.  His food was put on the ground and he
had no alternative except to seize it as best he
could, with his lips and teeth, while he held his
hands behind on his back.  Occasionally he could
be fed by another person who helped him to his
food with outstretched arms so as not to touch the
unfortunate one himself, but this assistant was
then in turn subjected to almost equally oppressive restrictions.  Almost every village contained some altogether disreputable individual,
ostracised by society, whose wretched existence
depended upon people's charity.  This creature
alone was allowed within arm's length of a person who had fulfilled the last duty towards the
deceased.  But as soon as the period of segrega-
tion was over and the person rendered unclean
through the corpse could again mingle with his
fellow-beings, all the dishes which he had used
during the dangerous period were broken and all
his clothing was thrown away.

The taboo customs after bodily contact with
the dead are the same all over Polynesia, in
Melanesia, and in a part of Africa; their most
constant feature is the prohibition against handling one's food and the consequent necessity of
being fed by somebody else.  It is noteworthy
that in Polynesia, or perhaps only in Hawaii,[36]

[36] Frazer, "Taboo," p. 138, etc.

priest-kings were subject to the same restrictions during the exercise of holy functions. In the taboo of the dead on the Island of Tonga the abatement and gradual abolition of the prohibitions through the individual's own taboo power are clearly shown. A person who touched the corpse of a dead chieftain was unclean for ten months; but if he was himself a chief, he was unclean for only three, four, or five months, according to the rank of the deceased; if it was the corpse of the idolized head-chief even the greatest chiefs became taboo for ten months. These savages are so certain that any one who violates these taboo rules must become seriously ill and die, that according to the opinion of an observer, they have never yet dared to convince themselves of the contrary.[37]

The taboo restrictions imposed upon persons whose contact with the dead is to be understood in the transferred sense, namely the mourning relatives such as widows and widowers, are essentially the same as those mentioned above, but they are of greater interest for the point we are trying to make. In the rules hitherto mentioned we see only the typical expression of the virulence and power of diffusion of the taboo; in those about to be cited we catch a gleam of

[37] W. Mariner, "The Natives of the Tonga Islands," 1818, see Frazer, l. c., p. 140.

the motives, including both the ostensible ones and those which may be regarded as the underlying and genuine motives.

Among the Shuswap in British-Columbia widows and widowers have to remain segregated during their period of mourning; they must not use their hands to touch the body or the head and all utensils used by them must not be used by any one else. No hunter will want to approach the hut in which such mourners live, for that would bring misfortune; if the shadow of one of the mourners should fall on him he would become ill. The mourners sleep on thorn bushes, with which they also surround their beds. This last precaution is meant to keep off the spirit of the deceased; plainer still is the reported custom of other North American tribes where the widow, after the death of her husband, has to wear a kind of trousers of dried grass in order to make herself inaccessible to the approach of the spirit. Thus it is quite obvious that touching "in the transferred sense" is after all understood only as bodily contact, since the spirit of the deceased does not leave his kin and does not desist from "hovering about them" during the period of mourning.

Among the Agutainos, who live on Palawan, one of the Philippine Islands, a widow may not leave her hut for the first seven or eight days

after her husband's death, except at night, when
she need not expect encounters. Whoever sees
her is in danger of immediate death and therefore she herself warns others of her approach by
hitting the trees with a wooden stick with every
step she takes; these trees all wither. Another
observation explains the nature of the danger inherent in a widow. In the district of Mekeo,
British New Guinea, a widower forfeits all civil
rights and lives like an outlaw. He may not tend
a garden, or show himself in public, or enter the
village or go on the street. He slinks about like
an animal, in the high grass or in the bushes, and
must hide in a thicket if he sees anybody, especially a woman, approaching. This last hint
makes it easy for us to trace back the danger of
the widower or widow to the danger of temptation. The husband who has lost his wife must
evade the desire for a substitute; the widow has
to contend with the same wish and beside this, she
may arouse the desire of other men because she
is without a master. Every such satisfaction
through a substitute runs contrary to the intention of mourning and would cause the anger of
the spirit to flare up.[38]

38 The same patient whose "impossibilities" I have correlated
with taboo, (see above, p. 47) acknowledged that she always
became indignant when she met anybody on the street who was
dressed in mourning. "Such people should be forbidden to go
out!" she said.

One of the most surprising, but at the same
time one of the most instructive taboo customs
of mourning among primitive races is the prohibition against pronouncing the *name* of the deceased. This is very widespread, and has been
subjected to many modifications with important
consequences.

Aside from the Australians and the Polynesians, who usually show us taboo customs in their
best state of preservation, we also find this prohibition among races so far apart and unrelated
to each other as the Samojedes in Siberia and
the Todas in South India, the Mongolians of
Tartary and the Tuaregs of the Sahara, the Aino
of Japan and the Akamba and Nandi in Central
Africa, the Tinguanes in the Philippines and the
inhabitants of the Nikobari Islands and of Madagascar and Borneo.[39] Among some of these
races the prohibition and its consequences hold
good only for the period of mourning while in
others it remains permanent; but in all cases it
seems to diminish with the lapse of time after the
death.

The avoidance of the name of the deceased is
as a rule kept up with extraordinary severity.
Thus, among many South American tribes, it is
considered the gravest insult to the survivors to
pronounce the name of the deceased in their pres-

[39] Frazer, l. c., p. 353.

ence, and the penalty set for it is no less than
that for the slaying itself.[40]   At first it is not easy
to guess why the mention of the name should be
so abominated, but the dangers associated with
it have called into being a whole series of interesting and important expedients to avoid this.
Thus the Masai in Africa have hit upon the eva-
sion of changing the name of the deceased immediately upon his death; he may now be mentioned without dread by this new name, while all
the prohibitions remain attached to the old name.
It seems to be assumed that the ghost does not
know his new name and will not find it out.   The
Australian tribes on Adelaide and Encounter
Bay are so consistently cautious that when a
death occurs almost every person who has the
same name as the deceased or a very similar one,
exchanges it for another.   Sometimes by a further extension of the same idea as seen among
several tribes in Victoria and in North America
all the relatives of the deceased change their
names regardless of whether their names resemble
the name of the deceased in sound.   Among the
Guaycuru in Paraguay the chief used to give
new names to all the members of the tribe, on
such sad occasions, which they then remembered
as if they had always had them.[41]

[40] Frazer, l. c., p. 352, etc.
[41] Frazer, l. c., p. 357, according to an old Spanish observer,
1732.

Furthermore, if the deceased had the same name as an animal or object, etc. some of the races just enumerated thought it necessary to give these animals and objects new names, in order not to be reminded of the deceased when they mentioned them. Through this there must have resulted a never ceasing change of vocabulary, which caused a good deal of difficulty for the missionaries, especially where the interdiction upon a name was permanent. In the seven years which the missionary Dobrizhofer spent among the Abipons in Paraguay, the name for jaguar was changed three times and the words for crocodile, thorns and animal slaughter underwent a similar fate.[42] But the dread of pronouncing a name which has belonged to a deceased person extends also to the mention of everything in which the deceased had any part, and a further important result of this process of suppression is that these races have no tradition or any historical reminiscences, so that we encounter the greatest difficulties in investigating their past history. Among a number of these primitive races compensating customs have also been established in order to re-awaken the names of the deceased after a long period of mourning; they are bestowed upon children, who were regarded as reincarnations of the dead.

42 Frazer, l. c., p. 360.

The strangeness of this taboo on names dimin-
ishes if we bear in mind that the savage looks
upon his name as an essential part and an important possession of his personality, and that he
ascribes the full significance of things to words.
Our children do the same, as I have shown elsewhere, and therefore they are never satisfied with
accepting a meaningless verbal similarity, but
consistently conclude that when two things have
identical names a deeper correspondence between
them must exist. Numerous peculiarities of
normal behavior may lead civilized man to conclude that he too is not yet as far removed as he
thinks from attributing the importance of things
to mere names and feeling that his name has become peculiárly identified with his person. This
is corroborated by psychoanalytic experiences,
where there is much occasion to point out the importance of names in unconscious thought activity.[43]    As was to be expected, the compulsion
neurotics behave just like savages in regard to
names. They show the full "complex sensitiveness" towards the utterance and hearing of special words (as do also other neurotics) and derive a good many, often serious, inhibitions from
their treatment of their own name. One of these
taboo patients, whom I knew, had adopted the
avoidance of writing down her name for fear that

[43] Stekel, Abraham.

it might get into somebody's hands who thus
would come into possession of a piece of her personality. In her frenzied faithfulness, which
she needed to protect herself against the temptations of her phantasy, she had created for herself
the commandment, "not to give away anything
of her personality." To this belonged first of all
her name, then by further application her hand-
writing, so that she finally gave up writing.

Thus it no longer seems strange to us that savages should consider a dead person's name as a
part of his personality and that it should be subjected to the same taboo as the deceased. Call-
ing a dead person by name can also be traced back
to contact with him, so that we can turn our attention to the more inclusive problem of why this
contact is visited with such a severe taboo.

The nearest explanation would point to the
natural horror which a corpse inspires, especially
in view of the changes so soon noticeable after
death. Mourning for a dead person must also
be considered as a sufficient motive for everything
which has reference to him. But horror of the
corpse evidently does not cover all the details of
taboo rules, and mourning can never explain to
us why the mention of the dead is a severe insult
to his survivors. On the contrary, mourning
loves to preoccupy itself with the deceased, to
elaborate his memory, and preserve it for

the longest possible time. Something besides
mourning must be made responsible for the peculiarities of taboo customs, something which evidently serves a different purpose. It is this very
taboo on names which reveals this still unknown
motive, and if the customs did not tell us about
it we would find it out from the statements of
the mourning savages themselves.

For they do not conceal the fact that they fear
the presence and the return of the spirit of a
dead person; they practice a host of ceremonies
to keep him off and banish him.[44] They look
upon the mention of his name as a conjuration
which must result in his immediate presence.[45]
They therefore consistently do everything to
avoid conjuring and awakening a dead person.
They disguise themselves in order that the spirit
may not recognize them,[46] they distort either his
name or their own, and become infuriated when
a ruthless stranger incites the spirit against his
survivors by mentioning his name. We can
hardly avoid the conclusion that they suffer, according to Wundt's expression, from the fear
of "his soul now turned into a demon." [47]

[44] Frazer, l. c., p. 353, cites the Tuaregs of the Sahara as an
example of such an acknowledgment.
[45] Perhaps this condition is to be added: as long as any part of
his physical remains exist. Frazer, l. c., p. 372.
[46] "On the Nikobar Islands," Frazer, l. c., p. 382.
[47] Wundt, "Religion and Myth," Vol. II, p. 49.

With this understanding we approach Wundt's conception who, as we have heard, sees the nature of taboo in the fear of demons.

The assumption which this theory makes, namely, that immediately after death the beloved member of a family becomes a demon, from whom the survivors have nothing but hostility to expect, so that they must protect themselves by every means from his evil desires, is so peculiar that our first impulse is not to believe it. Yet almost all competent authors agree as to this interpretation of primitive races. Westermarck,[48] who, in my opinion, gives altogether too little consideration to taboo, makes this statement: "On the whole facts lead me to conclude that the dead are more frequently regarded as enemies than as friends and that Jevons and Grant Allen are wrong in their assertion that it was formerly believed that the malevolence of the dead was as a rule directed only against strangers, while they were paternally concerned about the life and

[48] "The Origin and Development of Moral Conceptions," see section entitled "Attitude Towards the Dead," Vol. II, p. 424. Both the notes and the text show an abundance of corroborating, and often very characteristic testimony, e. g., the Maori believed that "the nearest and most beloved relatives changed their nature after death and bore ill-will even to their former favorites." The Austral negroes believe that every dead person is for a long time malevolent; the closer the relationship the greater the fear. The Central Eskimos are dominated by the idea that the dead come to rest very late and that at first they are to be feared as mischievous spirits who frequently hover about the village to spread illness, death and other evils. (Boas.)

welfare of their descendants and the members
of their clan."

R. Kleinpaul has written an impressive book
in which he makes use of the remnants of the old
belief in souls among civilized races to show the
relation between the living and the dead.[49]  According to him too, this relation culminates in the
conviction that the dead, thirsting for blood,
draw the living after them.  The living did not
feel themselves safe from the persecutions of
the dead until a body of water had been put
between them.  That is why it was preferred
to bury the dead on islands or to bring them
to the other side of a river, the expressions "here"
and "beyond" originated in this way.  Later
moderation has restricted the malevolence of
the dead to those categories where a peculiar
right to feel rancor had to be admitted, such as
the murdered who pursue their murderer as evil
spirits, and those who, like brides, had died with
their longings unsatisfied.  Kleinpaul believes
that originally, however, the dead were all vam-
pires, who bore ill-will to the living, and strove
to harm them and deprive them of life.  It was
the corpse that first furnished the conception of
an evil spirit.

The hypothesis that those whom we love best

49 R. Kleinpaul: "The Living and the Dead in Folklore, Religion and Myth," 1898.

turn into demons after death obviously allows us
to put a further question. What prompted
primitive races to ascribe such a change of senti-
ment to the beloved dead? Why did they make
demons out of them? According to Westermarck this question is easily answered.[50]  "As
death is usually considered the worst calamity
that can overtake man, it is believed that the
deceased are very dissatisfied with their lot.
Primitive races believe that death comes only
through being slain, whether by violence or by
magic, and this is considered already sufficient
reason for the soul to be vindictive and irritable.
The soul presumably envies the living and longs
for the company of its former kin; we can therefore understand that the soul should seek to kill
them with diseases in order to be re-united with
them. . . .

". . . A further explanation of the malevolence ascribed to souls lies in the instinctive fear
of them, which is itself the result of the fear of
death."

Our study of psychoneurotic disturbances
points to a more comprehensive explanation
which includes that of Westermarck.

When a wife loses her husband, or a daughter
her mother, it not infrequently happens that the
survivor is afflicted with tormenting scruples,

[50] l. c., p. 426.

called "obsessive reproaches" which raise the question whether she herself has not been guilty through carelessness or neglect, of the death of the beloved person. No recalling of the care with which she nursed the invalid, or direct refutation of the asserted guilt can put an end to the torture, which is the pathological expression of mourning and which in time slowly subsides. Psychoanalytic investigation of such cases has made us acquainted with the secret mainsprings of this affliction. We have ascertained that these obsessive reproaches are in a certain sense justified and therefore are immune to refutation or objections. Not that the mourner has really been guilty of the death or that she has really been careless, as the obsessive reproach asserts; but still there was something in her, a wish of which she herself was unaware, which was not displeased with the fact that death came, and which would have brought it about sooner had it been strong enough. The reproach now reacts against this unconscious wish after the death of the beloved person. Such hostility, hidden in the unconscious behind tender love, exists in almost all cases of intensive emotional allegiance to a particular person, indeed it represents the classic case, the prototype of the ambivalence of human emotions. There is always more or less of this ambivalence in everybody's disposition;

normally it is not strong enough to give rise to the obsessive reproaches we have described. But where there is abundant predisposition for it, it manifests itself in the relation to those we love most, precisely where you would least expect it. The disposition to compulsion neurosis, which we have so often taken for comparison with taboo problems, is distinguished by a particularly high degree of this original ambivalence of emotion.

We now know how to explain the supposed demonism of recently departed souls and the necessity of being protected against their hostility through taboo rules. By assuming a similar high degree of ambivalence in the emotional life of primitive races such as psychoanalysis ascribes to persons suffering from compulsion neurosis, it becomes comprehensible that the same kind of reaction against the hostility latent in the unconscious behind the obsessive reproaches of the neurotic should also be necessary here after the painful loss has occurred. But this hostility, which is painfully felt in the unconscious in the form of satisfaction with the demise, experiences a different fate in the case of primitive man: the defense against it is accomplished by displacement upon the object of hostility, namely the dead. We call this defense process, frequent both in normal and diseased psychic life, a *pro-*

*jection*. The survivor will deny that he has ever entertained hostile impulses toward the beloved dead; but now the soul of the deceased entertains them and will try to give vent to them during the entire period of mourning. In spite of the successful defense through projection, the punitive and remorseful character of this emotional reaction manifests itself in being afraid, in self-imposed renunciations and in subjection to restrictions which are partly disguised as protective measures against the hostile demon. Thus we find again that taboo has grown out of the soil of an ambivalent emotional attitude. The taboo of the dead also originates from the opposition between the conscious grief and the unconscious satisfaction at death. If this is the origin of the resentment of spirits it is self-evident that just the nearest and formerly most beloved survivors have to fear it most.

As in neurotic symptoms, the taboo regulations also evince opposite feelings. Their restrictive character expresses mourning, while they also betray very clearly what they are trying to conceal, namely, the hostility towards the dead, which is now motivated as self-defense. We have learnt to understand part of the taboo regulations as temptation fears. A dead person is defenseless, which must act as an incitement to satisfy hostile desires entertained against him;

this temptation has to be opposed by the prohibition.

But Westermarck is right in not admitting any difference in the savage's conception between those who have died by violence and those who have died a natural death. As will be shown later,[51] in the unconscious mode of thinking even a natural death is perceived as murder; the person was killed by evil wishes. Any one interested in the origin and meaning of dreams dealing with the death of dear relatives such as parents and brothers and sisters will find that the same feeling of ambivalence is responsible for the fact that the dreamer, the child, and the savage all have the same attitude towards the dead.[52]

A little while ago we challenged Wundt's conception, who explains the nature of taboo through the fear of demons, and yet we have just agreed with the explanation which traces back the taboo of the dead to a fear of the soul of the dead after it has turned into a demon. This seems like a contradiction, but it will not be difficult for us to explain it. It is true that we have accepted the idea of demons, but we know that this assumption is not something final which psychology cannot resolve into further elements. We have, as it were, exposed the demons by recognizing them

[51] Cf. Chap. III.
[52] Freud, "The Interpretation of Dreams."

as mere projections of hostile feelings which the survivor entertains towards the dead.

The double feeling—tenderness and hostility —against the deceased, which we consider well founded, endeavors to assert itself at the time of bereavement as mourning and satisfaction. A conflict must ensue between these contrary feelings and as one of them, namely the hostility, is altogether or for the greater part unconscious, the conflict cannot result in a conscious difference in the form of hostility or tenderness as, for instance, when we forgive an injury inflicted upon us by some one we love. The process usually adjusts itself through a special psychic mechanism, which is designated in psychoanalysis as *projection*. This unknown hostility, of which we are ignorant and of which we do not wish to know, is projected from our inner perception into the outer world and is thereby detached from our own person and attributed to the other. Not we, the survivors, rejoice because we are rid of the deceased, on the contrary, we mourn for him; but now, curiously enough, he has become an evil demon who would rejoice in our misfortune and who seeks our death. The survivors must now defend themselves against this evil enemy; they are freed from inner oppression, but they have only succeeded in exchanging it for an affliction from without.

It is not to be denied that this process of projection, which turns the dead into malevolent
enemies, finds some support in the real hostilities
of the dead which the survivors remember and
with which they really can reproach the dead.
These hostilities are harshness, the desire to dominate, injustice, and whatever else forms the background of even the most tender relations between
men.   But the process cannot be so simple that
this factor alone could explain the origin of
demons by projeetion.   The offenses of the dead
certainly motivate in part the hostility of the survivors, but they would have been ineffective if
they had not given rise to this hostility and the
occasion of death would surely be the least suitable occasion for awakening the memory of the
reproaches which justly could have been brought
against the deceased.   We cannot dispense with
the unconscious hostility as the constant and
really impelling motive.   This hostile tendency
towards those nearest and dearest could remain
latent during their lifetime, that is to say, it could
avoid betraying itself to consciousness either
directly or indirectly through any substitutive
formation.   However, when the person who was
simultaneously loved and hated died, this was no
longer possible, and the conflict became acute.
The mourning originating from the enhanced
tenderness, became on the one hand more iutol-

erant of the latent hostility, while on the other
hand it could not tolerate that the latter should
not give origin to a feeling of pure gratification.
Thus there came about the repression of the unconscious hostility through projection, and the
formation of the ceremonial in which fear of punishment by demons finds expression. With the
termination of the period of mourning, the conflict also loses its acuteness so that the taboo of
the dead can be abated or sink into oblivion.

4

Having thus explained the basis on which the
very instructive taboo of the dead has grown up,
we must not miss the opportunity of adding a few
observations which may become important for the
understanding of taboo in general.

The projection of unconscious hostility upon
demons in the taboo of the dead is only a single
example from a whole series of processes to which
we must grant the greatest influence in the formation of primitive psychic life. In the foregoing
case the mechanism of projection is used to settle
an emotional conflict; it serves the same purpose
in a large number of psychic situations which lead
to neuroses. But projection is not specially created for the purpose of defense, it also comes into
being where there are no conflicts. The projection of inner perceptions to the outside is a primi-

tive mechanism which, for instance, also influences our sense perceptions, so that it normally has the greatest share in shaping our outer world. Under conditions that have not yet been sufficiently determined even inner perceptions of ideational and emotional processes are projected outwardly, like sense perceptions, and are used to shape the outer world, whereas they ought to remain in the inner world. This is perhaps genetically connected with the fact that the function of attention was originally directed not towards the inner world, but to the stimuli streaming in from the outer world, and only received reports of pleasure and pain from the endopsychic processes. Only with the development of the language of abstract thought through the association of sensory remnants of word representations with inner processes, did the latter gradually become capable of perception. Before this took place primitive man had developed a picture of the outer world through the outward projection of inner perceptions, which we, with our reënforced conscious perception, must now translate back into psychology.

The projeetion of their own evil impulses upon demons is only a part of what has become the world system ("Weltanschauung") of primitive man which we shall discuss later as "animism." We shall then have to ascertain the psychological

nature of such a system formation and the points
of support which we shall find in the analysis
of these system formations will again bring us
face to face with the neurosis.  For the present
we merely wish to suggest that the "secondary
elaboration" of the dream content is the prototype of all these system formations.[53]   And let
us not forget that beginning at the stage of system formation there are two origins for every act
judged by consciousness, namely the systematic,
and the real but unconscious origin.[54]

Wundt [55] remarks that "among the influences
which myth everywhere ascribes to demons the
evil ones preponderate, so that according to the
religions of races evil demons are evidently older
than good demons."  Now it is quite possible
that the whole conception of demons was derived
from the extremely important relation to the
dead.  In the further course of human development the ambivalence inherent in this relation
then manifested itself by allowing two altogether
contrary psychic formations to issue from the
same root, namely, the fear of demons and of
*ghosts,* and the reverence for ancestors.[56]   Noth-

[53] Freud, "The Interpretation of Dreams."

[54] The projection creations of primitive man resemble the per-
sonifications through which the poet projects his warring impulses
out of himself, as separated individuals.

[55] "Myth and Religion," p. 129.

[56] In the psychoanalysis of neurotic persons who suffer, or have
suffered, in their childhood from the fear of ghosts, it is often not

ing testifies so much to the influence of mourning
on the origin of belief in demons as the fact that
demons were always taken to be the spirits of
persons not long dead. Mourning has a very distinct psychic task to perform, namely, to detach
the memories and expectations of the survivors
from the dead. When this work is accomplished
the grief, and with it the remorse and reproach,
lessens, and therefore also the fear of the demon.
But the very spirits which at first were feared as
demons now serve a friendlier purpose; they are
revered as ancestors and appealed to for help in
times of distress.

If we survey the relation of survivors to the
dead through the course of the ages, it is very evident that the ambivalent feeling has extraordinarily abated. We now find it easy to suppress
whatever unconscious hostility towards the dead
there may still exist without any special psychic
effort on our part. Where formerly satisfied
hate and painful tenderness struggled with each
other, we now find piety, which appears like a
cicatrice and demands: *De mortuis nil nisi bene.*
Only neurotics still blur the mourning for the loss
of their dear ones with attacks of compulsive re-

difficult to expose these ghosts as the parents. Compare also in
this connection the communication of P. Haeberlin, "Sexual
Ghosts" ("Sexual Problems," Feb., 1912), where it is a question
of another erotically accentuated person, but where the father was
dead.

proaches which psychoanalysis reveals as the old ambivalent emotional feeling. How this change was brought about, and to what extent constitutional changes and real improvement of familiar relations share in causing the abatement of the ambivalent feeling, need not be discussed here. But this example would lead us to assume *that the psychic impulses of primitive man possessed a higher degree of ambivalence than is found at present among civilized human beings. With the decline of this ambivalence the taboo, as the compromise symptom of the ambivalent conflict, also slowly disappeared.* Neurotics who are compelled to reproduce this conflict, together with the taboo resulting from it, may be said to have brought with them an atavistic remnant in the form of an archaic constitution the compensation of which in the interest of cultural demands entails the most prodigious psychic efforts on their part.

At this point we may recall the confusing information which Wundt offered us about the double meaning of the word taboo, namely, holy and unclean. (See above.) It was supposed that originally the word taboo did not yet mean holy and unclean but signified something demonic, something which may not be touched, thus emphasizing a characteristic common to both extremes of the later conception; this persistent

common trait proves, however, that an original
correspondence existed between what was holy
and what was unclean, which only later became
differentiated.

In contrast to this, our discussions readily show
that the double meaning in question belonged to
the word taboo from the very beginning and that
it serves to designate a definite ambivalence as
well as everything which has come into existence
on the basis of this ambivalence.  Taboo is itself
an ambivalent word and by way of supplement,
we may add that the established meaning of this
word might of itself have allowed us to guess
what we have found as the result of extensive investigation, namely, that the taboo prohibition is
to be explained as the result of an emotional
ambivalence.  A study of the oldest languages
has taught us that at one time there were many
such words which included their own contrasts
so that they were in a certain sense ambivalent,
though perhaps not exactly in the same sense as
the word taboo.[57]    Slight vocal modifications of
this primitive word containing two opposite
meanings later served to create a separate linguistic expression for the two opposites originally
united in one word.

[57] Compare my article on Abel's "Gegensinn des Urworte" in
the "Jahrbuch für Psychoanalytische und Psychopathologische
Forschungen," Bd. II, 1910.

The word taboo has had a different fate; with
the diminished importance of the ambivalence
which it connotes it has itself disappeared, or
rather, the words analogous to it have vanished
from the vocabulary.  In a later connection I
hope to be able to show that a tangible historic
change is probably concealed behind the fate of
this conception; that the word at first was associated with definite human relations which were
characterized by great emotional ambivalence
from which it expanded to other analogous relations.

Unless we are mistaken, the understanding of
taboo also throws light upon the nature and
origin of conscience.  Without stretching ideas
we can speak of a taboo conscience and a taboo
sense of guilt after the violation of a taboo.
Taboo conscience is probably the oldest form in
which we meet the phenomenon of conscience.

For what is "conscience"?  According to
linguistic testimony it belongs to what we know
most surely; in some languages its meaning is
hardly to be distinguished from consciousness.

Conscience is the inner perception of objections
to definite wish impulses that exist in us; but the
emphasis is put upon the fact that this rejection
does not have to depend on anything else, that it
is sure of itself.  This becomes even plainer in
the case of a guilty conscience, where we become

aware of the inner condemnation of such acts which realized some of our definite wish impulses. Confirmation seems superfluous here; whoever has a conscience must feel in himself the justification of the condemnation, and the reproach for the accomplished action. But this same character is evinced by the attitude of savages towards taboo. Taboo is a command of conscience, the violation of which causes a terrible sense of guilt which is as self-evident as its origin is unknown.[58]

It is therefore probable that conscience also originates on the basis of an ambivalent feeling from quite definite human relations which contain this ambivalence. It probably originates under conditions which are in force both for taboo and the compulsion neurosis, that is, one component of the two contrasting feelings is unconscious and is kept repressed by the compulsive domination of the other component. This is confirmed by many things which we have learned from our analysis of neuroses. In the first place the character of compulsion neurotics shows a predominant trait of painful conscientiousness which is a symptom of reaction against the temptation

[58] It is an interesting parallel that the sense of guilt resulting from the violation of a taboo is in no way diminished if the violation took place unwittingly (see examples above), and that even in the Greek myth the guilt of Oedipus is not cancelled by the fact that it was incurred without his knowledge and will and even against them,

which lurks in the unconscious, and which develops into the highest degrees of guilty conscience as their illness grows worse.    Indeed, one
may venture the assertion that if the origin of
guilty conscience could not be discovered through
compulsion neurotic patients, there would be no
prospect of ever discovering it.    This task is successfully solved in the case of the individual neurotic, and we are confident of finding a similar solution in the case of races.

In the second place we cannot help noticing
that the sense of guilt contains much of the nature
of anxiety; without hesitation it may be described
as "conscience phobia."    But fear points to unconscious sources; The psychology of the neuroses taught us that when wish feelings undergo
repression their libido becomes transformed into
anxiety.    In addition we must bear in mind that
the sense of guilt also contains something unknown and unconscious, namely the motivation
for the rejection.    The character of anxiety in
the sense of guilt corresponds to this unknown
quantity.

If taboo expresses itself mainly in prohibitions
it may well be considered self-evident, without
remote proof from the analogy with neurosis
that it is based on a positive, desireful impulse.
For what nobody desires to do does not have to
be forbidden, and certainly whatever is expressly

forbidden must be an object of desire. If we applied this plausible theory to primitive races we would have to conclude that among their strongest temptations were desires to kill their kings and priests, to commit incest, to abuse their dead and the like. That is not very probable. And if we should apply the same theory to those cases in which we ourselves seem to hear the voice of conscience most clearly we would arouse the greatest contradiction. For there we would assert with the utmost certainty that we did not feel the slightest temptation to violate any of these commandments, as for example, the commandment: Thou shalt not kill, and that we felt nothing but repugnance at the very idea.

But if we grant the testimony of our conscience the importance it claims, then the prohibition— the taboo as well as our moral prohibitions—becomes superfluous, while the existence of a conscience, in turn, remains unexplained and the connection between conscience, taboo and neurosis disappears. The net result of this would then be our present state of understanding unless we view the problem psychoanalytically.

But if we take into account the following results of psychoanalysis, our understanding of the problem is greatly advanced. The analysis of dreams of normal individuals has shown that our own temptation to kill others is stronger and more

frequent than we had suspected and that it produces psychic effects even where it does not reveal
itself to our consciousness. And when we have
learnt that the obsessive rules of certain neurotics
are nothing but measures of self-reassurance and
self-punishment erected against the reënforced
impulse to commit murder, we can return with
fresh appreciation to our previous hypothesis that
every prohibition must conceal a desire. We can
then assume that this desire to murder actually
exists and that the taboo as well as the moral prohibition are psychologically by no means superfluous but are, on the contrary, explained and
justified through our ambivalent attitude towards
the impulse to slay.

The nature of this ambivalent relation so often
emphasized as fundamental, namely, that the
positive underlying desire is unconscious, opens
the possibility of showing further connections and
explaining further problems. The psychic
processes in the unconscious are not entirely identical with those known to us from our conscious
psychic life, but have the benefit of certain notable
liberties of which the latter are deprived. An
unconscious impulse need not have originated
where we find it expressed, it can spring from an
entirely different place and may originally have
referred to other persons and relations, but
through the mechanism of *displacement,* it

reaches the point where it comes to our notice. Thanks to the indestructibility of unconscious processes and their inaccessibility to correction, the impulse may be saved over from earlier times to which it was adapted to later periods and conditions in which its manifestations must necessarily seem foreign.   These are all only hints, but a careful elaboration of them would show how important they may become for the understanding of the development of civilization.

In closing these discussions we do not want to neglect to make an observation that will be of use for later investigations.   Even if we insist upon the essential similarity between taboo and moral prohibitions we do not dispute that a psychological difference must exist between them.   A change in the relations of the fundamental ambivalence can be the only reason why the probibition no longer appears in the form of a taboo.

In the analytical consideration of taboo phenomena we have hitherto allowed ourselves to be guided by their demonstrable agreements with compulsion neurosis; but as taboo is not a neurosis but a social creation we are also confronted with the task of showing wherein lies the essential difference between the neurosis and a product of culture like the taboo.

Here again I will take a single fact as my starting point.   Primitive races fear a punishment for

the violation of a taboo, usually a serious disease
or death.   This punishment threatens only him
who has been guilty of the violation.   It is different with the compulsion neurosis.   If the patient
wants to do something that is forbidden to him
he does not fear punishment for himself, but for
another person.   This person is usually indefi-
nite, but, by means of analysis, is easily recognized as some one very near and dear to the patient.   The neurotic therefore acts as if he were
altruistic, while primitive man seems egotistical.
Only if retribution fails to overtake the taboo violator spontaneously does a collective feeling
awaken among savages that they are all threatened through the sacrilege, and they hasten to in-
flict the omitted punishment themselves.   It is
easy for us to explain the mechanism of this
solidarity.   It is a question of fear of the contagious example, the temptation to imitate, that is
to say, of the capacity of the taboo to infect.   If
some one has succeeded in satisfying the repressed
desire, the same desire must manifest itself in all
his companions; hence, in order to keep down this
temptation, this envied individual must be de-
spoiled of the fruit of his daring.   Not infrequently the punishment gives the executors themselves an opportunity to commit the same sacri-
legious act by justifying it as an expiation.   This
is really one of the fundamentals of the human

code of punishment which rightly presumes the same forbidden impulses in the criminal and in the members of society who avenge his offense.

Psychoanalysis here confirms what the pious were wont to say, that we are all miserable sinners. How then shall we explain the unexpected nobility of the neurosis which fears nothing for itself and everything for the beloved person? Psychoanalytic investigation shows that this nobility is not primary. Originally, that is to say at the beginning of the disease, the threat of punishment pertained to one's own person; in every case the fear was for one's own life; the fear of death being only later displaced upon another beloved person. The process is somewhat complicated but we have a complete grasp of it. An evil impulse—a death wish—towards the beloved person is always at the basis of the formation of a prohibition. This is repressed through a prohibition, and the prohibition is connected with a certain act which by displacement usually substitutes the hostile for the beloved person, and the execution of this act is threatened with the penalty of death. But the process goes further and the original wish for the death of the beloved other person is then replaced by fear for his death. The tender altruistic trait of the neurosis therefore merely *compensates* for the opposite attitude of brutal egotism which is at the basis of it. If

we designate as social those emotional impulses
which are determined through regard for another
person who is not taken as a sexual object, we can
emphasize the withdrawal of these social factors
as an essential feature of the neurosis, which is
later disguised through over-compensation.

Without lingering over the origin of these
social impulses and their relation to other fundamental impulses of man, we will bring out the second main characteristic of the neurosis by means
of another example.  The form in which taboo
manifests itself has the greatest similarity to the
touching phobia of neurotics, the *Délire de
toucher*.  As a matter of fact this neurosis is regularly concerned with the prohibition of sexual
touching and psychoanalysis has quite generally
shown that the motive power which is deflected
and displaced in the neurosis is of sexual origin.
In taboo the forbidden contact has evidently not
only sexual significance but rather the more general one of attack, of acquisition and of personal
assertion.  If it is prohibited to touch the chief
or something that was in contact with him it
means that an inhibition should be imposed upon
the same impulse which on other occasions expresses itself in suspicious surveillance of the
chief and even in physical ill-treatment of him
before his coronation.  (See above.)  *Thus the
preponderance of sexual components of the im-*

*pulse over the social components is the determining factor of the neurosis.* But the social impulses themselves came into being through the union of egotistical and erotic components into special entities.

From this single example of a comparison between taboo and compulsion neurosis it is already possible to guess the relation between individual forms of the neurosis and the creations of culture, and in what respect the study of the psychology of the neurosis is important for the understanding of the development of culture.

In one way the neuroses show a striking and far-reaching correspondence with the great social productions of art, religion and philosophy, while again they seem like distortions of them. We may say that hysteria is a caricature of an artistic creation, a compulsion neurosis, a caricature of a religion, and a paranoic delusion a caricature of a philosophic system. In the last analysis this deviation goes back to the fact that the neuroses are asocial formations; they seek to accomplish by private means what arose in society through collective labor. In analyzing the impulse of the neuroses one learns that motive powers of sexual origin exercise the determining influence in them, while the corresponding cultural creations rest upon social impulses and on such as have issued from the combination of egotistical and sexual components.   It seems that the sexual need is not capable of uniting men in the same way as the demands of self preservation; sexual satisfaction is in the first place the private concern of the individual.

Genetically the asocial nature of the neurosis springs from its original tendency to flee from a dissatisfying reality to a more pleasurable world of phantasy.  This real world which neurotics shun is dominated by the society of human beings and by the institutions created by them; the estrangement from reality is at the same time a withdrawal from human companionship.

# CHAPTER III

## 1

It is a necessary defect of studies which seek to apply the point of view of psychoanalysis to the mental sciences that they cannot do justice to either subject. They therefore confine themselves to the rôle of incentives and make suggestions to the expert which he should take into consideration in his work. This defect will make itself felt most strongly in an essay such as this which tries to treat of the enormous sphere called animism.[1]

Animism in the narrower sense is the theory of psychic concepts and in the wider sense, of spiritual beings in general. Animatism, the animation theory of seemingly inanimate nature, is a further subdivision which also includes animatism

---

1 The necessary crowding of the material also compels us to dispense with a thorough bibliography. Instead of this the reader is referred to the well-known works of Herbert Spencer, J. G. Frazer, A. Lang, E. B. Tylor and W. Wundt, from which all the statements concerning animism and magic are taken. The independence of the author can manifest itself only in the choice of the material and of opinions.

and animism. The name animism, formerly applied to a definite philosophic system, seems to
have acquired its present meaning through E. B.
Tylor.[2]

What led to the formulation of these names is
the insight into the very remarkable conceptions
of nature and the world of those primitive races
known to us from history and from our own
times. These races populate the world with a
multitude of spiritual beings which are benevolent
or malevolent to them, and attribute the causation
of natural processes to these spirits and demons;
they also consider that not only animals and
plants, but inanimate things as well are animated
by them. A third and perhaps the most important part of this primitive "nature philosophy"
seems far less striking to us because we ourselves
are not yet far enough removed from it, though
we have greatly limited the existence of spirits
and to-day explain the processes of nature by the
assumption of impersonal physical forces. For
primitive people believe in a similar "animation"
of human individuals as well. Human beings
have souls which can leave their habitation and
enter into other beings; these souls are the bearers
of spiritual activities and are, to a certain extent,
independent of the "bodies." Originally souls

2 E. B. Tylor, "Primitive Culture," Vol. I, p. 425, fourth ed.,
1903. W. Wundt, "Myth and Religion," Vol. II, p. 173, 1906.

were thought of as being very similar to individuals; only in the course of a long evolution did they lose their material character and attain a high degree of "spiritualization." [3]

Most authors incline to the assumption that these soul conceptions are the original nucleus of the animistic system, that spirits merely correspond to souls that have become independent, and that the souls of animals, plants and things were formed after the analogy of human souls.

How did primitive people come to the peculiarly dualistic fundamental conceptions on which this animistic system rests? Through the observation, it is thought, of the phenomena of sleep (with dreams) and death which resemble sleep, and through the effort to explain these conditions, which affect each individual so intimately. Above all, the problem of death must have become the starting point of the formation of the theory. To primitive man the continuation of life—immortality—would be self-evident. The conception of death is something accepted later, and only with hesitation, for even to us it is still devoid of content and unrealizable. Very likely discussions have taken place over the part which may have been played by other observations and experiences in the formation of the fundamental animistic conceptions such as dream

[3] Wundt l. c., Chapter IV, "Die Seelenvorstellungen."

imagery, shadows and reflections, but these have led to no conclusion.[4]

If primitive man reacted to the phenomena that stimulated his reflection with the formation of conceptions of the soul, and then transferred these to objects of the outer world, his attitude will be judged to be quite natural and in no way mysterious. In view of the fact that animistic conceptions have been shown to be similar among the most varied races and in all periods, Wundt states that these "are the necessary psychological product of the myth forming consciousness, and primitive animism may be looked upon as the spiritual expression of man's natural state in so far as this is at all accessible to our observation." [5] Hume has already justified the animation of the inanimate in his "Natural History of Religions," where he said: "There is a universal tendency among mankind to conceive all beings like themselves and to transfer to every object those qualities with which they are familiarly acquainted and of which they are intimately conscious." [6]

Animism is a system of thought, it gives not only the explanation of a single phenomenon, but makes it possible to comprehend the totality of

[4] Compare, besides Wundt and H. Spencer and the instructive article in the "Encyclopedia Britannica," 1911 (Animism, Mythology, and so forth).

[5] l. c., p. 154.

[6] See Tylor, "Primitive Culture," Vol. I, p. 477.

the world from one point, as a continuity.  Writers maintain that in the course of time three such systems of thought, three great world systems came into being: the animistic (mythological), the religious, and the scientific.  Of these animism, the first system is perhaps the most consistent and the most exhaustive, and the one which explains the nature of the world in its entirety.  This first world system of mankind is now a psychological theory.  It would go beyond our scope to show how much of it can still be demonstrated in the life of to-day, either as a worthless survival in the form of superstition, or in living form, as the foundation of our language, our belief, and our philosophy.

It is in reference to the successive stages of these three world systems that we say that animism in itself was not yet a religion but contained the prerequisites from which religions were later formed.  It is also evident that myths are based upon animistic foundations, but the detailed relation of myths to animism seem unexplained in some essential points.

## 2

Our psychoanalytic work will begin at a different point.  It must not be assumed that mankind came to create its first world system through a purely speculative thirst for knowledge.  The practical need of mastering the world must have contributed to this effort. We are therefore not astonished to learn that something else went hand in hand with the animistic system, namely the elaboration of directions for making oneself master of men, animals and things, as well as of their spirits. S. Reinach [7] wants to call these directions, which are known under the names of "sorcery and magic," the strategy of animism; With Mauss and Hubert, I should prefer to compare them to a technique.[8]

Can the conceptions of sorcery and magic be separated? It can be done if we are willing on our own authority to put ourselves above the vagaries of linguistic usage. Then sorcery is essentially the art of influencing spirits by treating them like people under the same circumstances, that is to say by appeasing them, reconciling them, making them more favorably disposed to one, by intimidating them, by depriving them of their power and by making them subject to one's will; all that is accomplished through the same methods that have been found effective with living people. Magic, however, is something else; it does not essentially concern itself with spirits, and uses special means, not the ordinary

[7] "Cultes, Mythes et Religions," T. II, Introduction, p. XV, 1909.
[8] "Année Sociologique," Seventh Vol., 1904.

psychological method. We can easily guess that magic is the earlier and the more important part of animistic technique, for among the means with which spirits are to be treated there are also found the magic kind,[9] and magic is also applied where spiritualization of nature has not yet, as it seems to us, been accomplished.

Magic must serve the most varied purposes. It must subject the processes of nature to the will of man, protect the individual against enemies and dangers, and give him the power to injure his enemies. But the principles on whose assumptions the magic activity is based, or rather the principle of magic, is so evident that it was recognized by all authors. If we may take the opinion of E. B. Tylor at its face value it can be most tersely expressed in his words: "mistaking an ideal connection for a real one." We shall explain this characteristic in the case of two groups of magic acts.

One of the most widespread magic procedures for injuring an enemy consists of making an effigy of him out of any kind of material. The likeness counts for little, in fact any object may be "named" as his image. Whatever is subsequently done to this image will also happen to

---

[9] To frighten away a ghost with noise and cries is a form of pure sorcery; to force him to do something by taking his name is to employ magic against him,

the hated prototype; thus if the effigy has been injured in any place he will be afflicted by a disease in the corresponding part of the body.    This same magic technique, instead of being used for private enmity can also be employed for pious purposes and can thus be used to aid the gods against evil demons.    I quote Frazer: [10]    "Every night when the sun-god Ra in ancient Egypt sank to his home in the glowing west he was assailed by hosts of demons under the leadership of the archfiend Apepi.    All night long he fought them, and sometimes by day the powers of darkness sent up clouds even into the blue Egyptian sky to obscure his light and weaken his power. To aid the sun-god in this daily struggle, a ceremony was daily performed in his temple at Thebes.    A figure of his foe Apepi, represented as a crocodile with a hideous face or a serpent with many coils, was made of wax, and on it the demon's name was written in green ink.    Wrapt in a papyrus case, on which another likeness of Apepi had been drawn in green ink, the figure was then tied up with black hair, spat upon, hacked with a stone knife and cast on the ground. There the priest trod on it with his left foot again and again, and then burned it in a fire made of a certain plant or grass.    When Apepi himself had thus been effectively disposed of, waxen effigies

10 " The Magic Art," II, p. 67.

of each of his principal demons, and of their
fathers, mothers, and children, were made and
burnt in the same way. The service, accompanied by the recitation of certain prescribed
spells, was repeated not merely morning, noon
and night, but whenever a storm was raging or
heavy rain had set in, or black clouds were steal-
ing across the sky to hide the sun's bright disk.
The fiends of darkness, clouds and rain, felt the
injury inflicted on their images as if it had been
done to themselves; they passed away, at least for
a time, and the beneficent sun-god shone out tri-
umphant once more." [11]

There is a great mass of magic actions which
show a similar motivation but I shall lay stress
upon only two, which have always played a great
rôle among primitive races and which have been
partly preserved in the myths and cults of higher
stages of evolution: the art of causing rain and
fruitfulness by magic. Rain is produced by
magic means, by imitating it, and perhaps also
by imitating the clouds and storm which produce
it. It looks as if they wanted to "play rain."
The Ainos of Japan, for instance, make rain by

[11] The Biblical prohibition against making an image of anything
living hardly sprang from any fundamental rejection of plastic
art, but was probably meant to deprive magic, which the Hebraic
religion proscribed, of one of its instruments. Frazer, l. c., p. 87,
note.

pouring out water through a big sieve, while others fit out a big bowl with sails and oars as if it were a ship, which is then dragged about the village and gardens. But the fruitfulness of the soil was assured by magic means by showing it the spectacle of human sexual intercourse. To cite one out of many examples; in some part of Java, the peasants used to go out into the fields at night for sexual intercourse when the rice was about to blossom in order to stimulate the rice to fruitfulness through their example.[12] At the same time it was feared that proscribed incestuous relationships would stimulate the soil to grow weeds and render it unfruitful.[13]

Certain negative rules, that is to say magic precautions, must be put into this first group. If some of the inhabitants of a Dayak village had set out on a hunt for wild-boars, those remaining behind were in the meantime not permitted to touch either oil or water with their hands, as such acts would soften the hunters' fingers and would let the quarry slip through their hands.[14] Or when a Gilyak hunter was pursuing game in the woods, his children were forbidden to make drawings on wood or in the sand, as the paths in the

12 "The Magic Art," II, p. 98.

13 An echo of this is to be found in the "Oedipus Rex" of Sophocles.

14 "The Magic Art," p. 120.

thick woods might become as intertwined as the lines of the drawing, and the hunter would not find his way home.[15]

The fact that in these as in a great many other examples of magic influence, distance plays no part, telepathy is taken as a matter of course—will cause us no difficulties in grasping the peculiarity of magic.

There is no doubt about what is considered the effective force in all these examples. It is the *similarity* between the performed action and the expected happening. Frazer therefore calls this kind of magic *imitative* or *homeopathic*. If I want it to rain I only have to produce something that looks like rain or recalls rain. In a later phase of cultural development, instead of these magic conjurations of rain, processions are arranged to a house of god, in order to supplicate the saint who dwells there to send rain. Finally also this religious technique will be given up and instead an effort will be made to find out what would influence the atmosphere to produce rain.

In another group of magic actions the principle of similarity is no longer involved, but in its stead there is another principle the nature of which is well brought out in the following examples.

Another method may be used to injure an

15 l. c., p. 122.

enemy. You possess yourself of his hair, his nails, anything that he has discarded, or even a part of his clothing, and do something hostile to these things. This is just as effective as if you had dominated the person himself, and anything that you do to the things that belong to him must happen to him too. According to the conception of primitive men a name is an essential part of a personality; if therefore you know the name of a person or a spirit you have acquired a certain power over its bearer. This explains the remarkable precautions and restrictions in the use of names which we have touched upon in the essay on taboo.[16] In these examples similarity is evidently replaced by relationship.

The cannibalism of primitive races derives its more sublime motivation in a similar manner. By absorbing parts of the body of a person through the act of eating we also come to possess the properties which belonged to that person. From this there follow precautions and restrictions as to diet under special circumstances. Thus a pregnant woman will avoid eating the meat of certain animals because their undesirable properties, for example, cowardice, might thus be transferred to the child she is nourishing. It makes no difference to the magic influence whether the connection is already abolished or

[16] See preceding chapter, p. 92.

whether it had consisted of only one very important contact. Thus, for instance, the belief
in a magic bond which links the fate of a wound
with the weapon which caused it can be followed
unchanged through thousands of years. If a
Melanesian gets possession of the bow by which
he was wounded he will carefully keep it in a cool
place in order thus to keep down the inflamma-
tion of the wound. But if the bow has remained
in the possession of the enemy it will certainly be
kept in close proximity to a fire in order that
the wound may burn and become thoroughly
inflamed. Pliny, in his Natural History
XXVIII, advises spitting on the hand which
has caused the injury if one regrets having injured some one; the pain of the injured person
will then immediately be eased. Francis Bacon,
in his Natural History, mentions the generally
accredited belief that putting a salve on the
weapon which has made a wound will cause this
wound to heal of itself. It is said that even to-
day English peasants follow this prescription,
and that if they have cut themselves with a scythe
they will from that moment on carefully keep the
instrument clean in order that the wound may
not fester. In June, 1902, a local English
weekly reported that a woman called Matilde
Henry of Norwich accidentally ran an iron nail
into the sole of her foot. Without having the

wound examined or even taking off her stocking
she bade her daughter to oil the nail thoroughly,
in the expectation that then nothing could happen to her. She died a few days later of
tetanus [17] in consequence of postponed antisepsis.

The examples from this last group illustrate
Frazer's distinction between *contagious* magic
and *imitative* magic. What is considered as
effective in these examples is no longer the similarity, but the association in space, the contiguity,
or at least the imagined contiguity, or the memory of its existence. But since similarity and
contiguity are the two essential principles of the
processes of association of ideas, it must be concluded that the dominance of associations of ideas
really explains all the madness of the rules of
magic. We can see how true Tylor's quoted
characteristic of magic: "mistaking an ideal connection for a real one," proves to be. The same
may be said of Frazer's idea, who has expressed
it in almost the same terms: "men mistook the
order of their ideas for the order of nature, and
hence imagined that the control which they have,
or seem to have, over their thoughts, permitted
them to have a corresponding control over
things." [18]

It will at first seem strange that this illuminat-

[17] Frazer, "The Magic Art," p. 201-203.
[18] "The Magic Art," p. 420.

ing explanation of magic could have been rejected by some authors as unsatisfactory.[19]
But on closer consideration we must sustain the
objection that the association theory of magic
merely explains the paths that magic travels, and
not its essential nature, that is, it does not explain the misunderstanding which bids it put
psychological laws in place of natural ones. We
are apparently in need here of a dynamic factor;
but while the search for this leads the critics of
Frazer's theory astray, it will be easy to give a
satisfactory explanation of magic by carrying
its association theory further and by entering
more deeply into it.

First let us examine the simpler and more important case of imitative magic. According to
Frazer this may be practiced by itself, whereas
contagious magic as a rule presupposes the imitative.[20] The motives which impel one to exercise magic are easily recognized; they are the
wishes of men. We need only assume that
primitive man had great confidence in the power
of his wishes. At bottom everything which he
accomplished by magic means must have been
done solely because he wanted it. Thus in the
beginning only his wish is accentuated.

[19] Compare the article "Magic" (N. T. W.) "Encyclopedia
Britannica, 11th Ed.
[20] l. c., p. 54.

In the case of the child which finds itself under analogous psychic conditions, without being as yet capable of motor activity, we have elsewhere advocated the assumption that it at first really satisfies its wishes by means of hallucinations, in that it creates the satisfying situation through centrifugal excitements of its sensory organs.[21] The adult primitive man knows another way. A motor impulse, the will, clings to his wish and this will which later will change the face of the earth in the service of wish fulfillment is now used to represent the gratification so that one may experience it, as it were, through motor hallucination. Such a *representation* of the gratified wish is altogether comparable to the *play* of children, where it replaces the purely sensory technique of gratification. If play and imitative representation suffice for the child and for primitive man, it must not be taken as a sign of modesty, in our sense, or of resignation due to the realization of their impotence, on the contrary, it is the very obvious result of the excessive valuation of their wish, of the will which depends upon the wish and of the paths the wish takes. In time the psychic accent is displaced from the motives of the magic act to its means, namely to the act itself. Perhaps it would be

[21] Formulation of two principles of psychic activity, "Jahrb. fur Psychoanalyt. Forschungen," Vol. III, 1912, p. 2.

more correct to say that primitive man does not become aware of the over-valuation of his psychic acts until it becomes evident to him through the means employed. It would also seem as if it were the magic act itself which compels the fulfillment of the wish by virtue of its similarity to the object desired. At the stage of animistic thinking there is as yet no way of demonstrating objectively the true state of affairs, but this becomes possible at later stages when, though such procedures are still practiced, the psychic phenomenon of skepticism already manifests itself as a tendency to repression. At that stage men will acknowledge that the conjuration of spirits avails nothing unless accompanied by belief, and that the magic effect of prayer fails if there is no piety behind it.[22]

The possibility of a contagious magic which depends upon contiguous association will then show us that the psychic valuation of the wish and the will has been extended to all psychic acts which the will can command. We may say that at present there is a general over-valuation of all psychic processes, that is to say there is an attitude towards the world which according to our understanding of the relation of reality to

---

[22] The King in "Hamlet" (Act III, Scene 4):
"My words fly up, my thoughts remain below,
Words without thoughts never to heaven go."

thought must appear like an over-estimation of the latter. Objects as such are over-shadowed by the ideas representing them; what takes place in the latter must also happen to the former and the relations which exist between ideas are also postulated as to things. As thought does not recognize distances and easily brings together in one act of consciousness things spatially and temporally far removed, the magic world also puts itself above spatial distance by telepathy, and treats a past association as if it were a present one. In the animistic age the reflection of the inner world must obscure that other picture of the world which we believe we recognize.

Let us also point out that the two principles of association, similarity and contiguity, meet in the higher unity of contact. Association by contiguity is contact in the direct sense, and association by similarity is contact in the transferred sense. Another identity in the psychic process which has not yet been grasped by us is probably concealed in the use of the same word for both kinds of associations. It is the same range of the concept of contact which we have found in the analysis of taboo.[23]

In summing up we may now say that the principle which controls magic, and the technique of

[23] Compare Chapter II.

the animistic method of thought, is "Omnipotence of Thought."

### 3

I have adopted the term "Omnipotence of Thought" from a highly intelligent man, a former sufferer from compulsion neurosis, who, after being cured through psychoanalytic treatment, was able to demonstrate his efficiency and good sense.[24] He had coined this phrase to designate all those peculiar and uncanny occurrenees which seemed to pursue him just as they pursue others afflicted with his malady. Thus if he happened to think of a person, he was actually confronted with this person as if he had conjured him up; if he inquired suddenly about the state of health of an acquaintance whom he had long missed he was sure to hear that this acquaintance had just died, so that he could believe that the deceased had drawn his attention to himself by telepathic means; if he uttered a half meant imprecation against a stranger, he could expect to have him die soon thereafter and burden him with the responsibility for his death. He was able to explain most of these cases in the course of the treatment, he could tell how the illusion had originated, and what he himself had

[24] Remarks upon a case of Compulsion Neurosis, "Jahrb. für Psychoanalyt. und Psychopath. Forschungen," Vol. I, 1909,

contributed towards furthering his superstitious expectations.[25] All compulsion neurotics are superstitious in this manner and often against their better judgment.

The existence of omnipotence of thought is most clearly seen in compulsion neurosis, where the results of this primitive method of thought are most often found or met in consciousness. But we must guard against seeing in this a distinguishing characteristic of this neurosis, for analytic investigation reveals the same mechanism in the other neuroses. In every one of the neuroses it is not the reality of the experience but the reality of the thought which forms the basis for the symptom formation. Neurotics live in a special world in which, as I have elsewhere expressed it, only the "neurotic standard of currency" counts, that is to say, only things intensively thought of or affectively conceived are effective with them, regardless of whether these things are in harmony with outer reality. The ysteric repeats in his attacks and fixates through his symptoms, occurrences which have taken place only in his phantasy, though in the last analysis they go back to real events or have been built up from them. The neurotic's guilty conscience is

25 We seem to attribute the character of the "uncanny" to all such impressions which seek to confirm the omnipotence of thought and the animistic method of thought in general, though our judgment has long rejected it.

just as incomprehensible if traced to real misdeeds. A compulsion neurotic may be oppressed
by a sense of guilt which is appropriate to a
wholesale murderer, while at the same time he
acts towards his fellow beings in a most consider-
ate and scrupulous manner, a behavior which he
evinced since his childhood. And yet his sense
of guilt is justified; it is based upon intensive and
frequent death wishes which unconsciously manifest themselves towards his fellow beings. It is
motivated from the point of view of unconscious
thoughts, but not of intentional acts. Thus the
omnipotence of thought, the over-estimation of
psychic processes as opposed to reality, proves to
be of unlimited effect in the neurotic's affective
life and in all that emanates from it. But if we
subject him to psychoanalytic treatment, which
makes his unconscious thoughts conscious to him,
he refuses to believe that thoughts are free and
is always afraid to express evil wishes lest
they be fulfilled in consequence of his utterance.
But through this attitude as well as through the
superstition which plays an active part in his life
he reveals to us how close he stands to the savage who believes he can change the outer world
by a mere thought of his.

The primary obsessive actions of these neurotics are really altogether of a magical nature.
If not magic they are at least anti-magic and are

destined to ward off the expectation of evil with which the neurosis is wont to begin. Whenever I was able to pierce these secrets it turned out that the content of this expectation of evil was death. According to Schopenhauer the problem of death stands at the beginning of every philosophy; we have heard that the formation of the soul conception and of the belief in demons which characterize animism, are also traced back to the impression which death makes upon man. It is hard to decide whether these first compulsive and protective actions follow the principle of similarity, or of contrast, for under the conditions of the neurosis they are usually distorted through displacement upon some trifle, upon some action which in itself is quite insignificant.[26] The protective formulas of the compulsion neurosis also have a counterpart in the incantations of magic. But the evolution of compulsive actions may be described by pointing out how these actions begin as a spell against evil wishes which are very remote from anything sexual, only to end up as a substitute for forbidden sexual activity, which they imitate as faithfully as possible.

If we accept the evolution of man's conceptions of the universe mentioned above, according to which the *animistic* phase is *succeeded* by the

[26] The following discussions will yield a further motive for this displacement upon a trivial action.

*religious,* and this in turn by the *scientific,* we have no difficulty in following the fortunes of the "omnipotence of thought" through all these phases. In the animistic stage man ascribes omnipotence to himself; in the religious he has ceded it to the gods, but without seriously giving it up, for he reserves to himself the right to control the gods by influencing them in some way or other in the interest of his wishes. In the scientific attitude towards life there is no longer any room for man's omnipotence; he has acknowledged his smallness and has submitted to death as to all other natural necessities in a spirit of resignation. Nevertheless, in our reliance upon the power of the human spirit which copes with the laws of reality, there still lives on a fragment of this primitive belief in the omnipotence of thought.

In retracing the development of libidinous impulses in the individual from its mature form back to its first beginnings in childhood, we at first found an important distinction which is stated in the "Three Contributions to the Theory of Sex." [27] The manifestations of sexual impulses can be recognized from the beginning but at first they are not yet directed to any outer object. Each individual component of the sexual impulse works for a gain in pleasure and finds its gratification in its own body. This stage

[27] Monograph Series, 1916.

is called *autoerotism* and is distinguished from
the stage of object selection.

In the course of further study it proved to be
practical and really necessary to insert a third
stage between these two or, if one prefers, to
divide the first stage of autoerotism into two. In
this intermediary stage, the importance of which
increases the more we investigate it, the sexual
impulses which formerly were separate, have already formed into a unit and have also found an
object; but this object is not external and foreign
to the individual, but is his own ego, which is
formed at this period. This new stage is called
*narcism,* in view of the pathological fixation of
this condition which may be observed later on.
The individual acts as if he were in love with
himself; for the purposes of our analysis the ego
impulses and the libidinous wishes cannot yet be
separated from each other.

Although this narcistic stage, in which the hitherto dissociated sexual impulses combine into a
unity and take the ego as their object, cannot as
yet be sharply differentiated, we can already
surmise that the narcistic organization is never
altogether given up again. To a certain extent
man remains narcistic, even after he has found
outer objects for his libido, and the objects upon
which he bestows it represent, as it were, emanations of the libido which remain with his ego and

which can be withdrawn into it. The state of
being in love, so remarkable psychologically, and
the normal prototype of the psychoses, corresponds to the highest stage of these emanations,
in contrast to the state of self-love.

This high estimation of psychic acts found
among primitives and neurotics, which we feel to
be an overestimation, may now appropriately be
brought into relation to narcism, and interpreted
as an essential part of it. We would say that
among primitive people thinking is still highly
sexualized and that this accounts for the belief
in the omnipotence of thought, the unshaken
confidence in the capacity to dominate the world
and the inaccessibility to the obvious facts which
could enlighten man as to his real place in the
world. In the case of neurotics a considerable
part of this primitive attitude has remained as
a constitutional factor, while on the other hand
the sexual repression occurring in them has
brought about a new sexualization of the processes of thought. In both cases, whether we deal
with an original libidinous investment of thought
or whether the same process has been accomplished regressively, the psychic results are the
same, namely, intellectual narcism and omnipotence of thought.[28]

[28] It is almost an axiom with writers on this subject, that a sort
of "Solipsism or Berkleianism" (as Professor Sully terms it as

If we may take the now established omnipotence of thought among primitive races as a proof of their narcism, we may venture to compare the various evolutionary stages of man's conception of the universe with the stages of the libidinous evolution of the individual. We find that the animistic phase corresponds in time as well as in content with narcism, the religious phase corresponds to that stage of object finding which is characterized by dependence on the parents, while the scientific stage has its full counterpart in the individual's state of maturity where, having renounced the pleasure principle and having adapted himself to reality, he seeks his object in the outer world.[29]

Only in one field has the omnipotence of thought been retained in our own civilization, namely in art. In art alone it still happens that man, consumed by his wishes, produces something similar to the gratification of these wishes and this playing, thanks to artistic illusion, calls forth affects as if it were something real. We rightly speak of the magic of art and compare the artist with a magician. But this comparison is

he finds it in the child) operates in the savage to make him refuse to recognize death as a fact.—Marett, "Pre-animistic Religion, Folklore," Vol. XI, 1900, p. 178.

[29] We merely wish to indicate here that the original narcism of the child is decisive for the interpretation of its character development and that it precludes the assumption of a primitive feeling of inferiority for the child.

perhaps more important than it claims to be. Art, which certainly did not begin as art for art's sake, originally served tendencies which to-day have for the greater part ceased to exist. Among these we may suspect various magic intentions.[30]

## 4

Animism, the first conception of the world which man succeeded in evolving, was therefore psychological. It did not yet require any science to establish it, for science sets in only after we have realized that we do not know the world and that we must therefore seek means of getting to know it. But animism was natural and self-evident to primitive man; he knew how the things of the world were constituted, and as man conceived himself to be. We are therefore prepared to find that primitive man transferred the struc-

[30] S. Reinach, "L'art et la Magie," in the collection, "Cultes, Mythes et Religions," Vol. I, p. 125-136. Reinach thinks that the primitive artists who have left us the scratched or painted animal pictures in the caves of France did not want to "arouse" pleasure, but to "conjure things." He explains this by showing that these drawings are in the darkest and most inaccessible part of the caves and that representations of feared beasts of prey are absent. "Les modernes parlent souvent, par hyperbole, de la magie du pinceau ou du ciseau d'un grand artiste et, en général, de la magie de l'art. Entendu en sense propre, qui est celui d'une contrainte mystique exercée par la volonté de l'homme sur d'autres volontés ou sur les choses, cette expression n'est plus admissible; mais nous avons vu qu'elle était autrefois rigouresement vraie, du moins dans l'opinion des artistes" (p. 136).

tural relations of his own psyche to the outer world,[31] and on the other hand we may make the attempt to transfer back into the human soul what animism teaches about the nature of things.

-Magic, the technique of animism, clearly and unmistakably shows the tendency of forcing the laws of psychic life upon the reality of things, under conditions where spirits did not yet have to play any rôle, and could still be taken as objects of magic treatment. The assumptions of magic are therefore of older origin than the spirit theory, which forms the nucleus of animism. Our psychoanalytic view here coincides with a theory of R. R. Marett, according to which animism is preceded by a pre-animistic stage the nature of which is best indicated by the name Animatism (the theory of general animation). We have practically no further knowledge of pre-animism, as no race has yet been found without conceptions of spirits.[32]

While magic still retains the full omnipotence of ideas, animism has ceded part of this omnipotence to spirits and thus has started on the way to form a religion. Now what could have moved primitive man to this first act of renunciation? It could hardly have been an insight into the in-

[31] Recognized through so-called endopsychic perceptions.

[32] R. R. Marett, "Pre-animistic Religion, Folklore," Vol. XI, No. 2, London, 1900.—Comp. Wundt, "Myth and Religion," Vol. II, p. 171.

correctness of his assumptions, for he continued to retain the magic technique.

As pointed out elsewhere, spirits and demons were nothing but the projection of primitive man's emotional impulses;[33] he personified the things he endowed with affects, populated the world with them and then rediscovered his inner psychic processes outside himself, quite like the ingenious paranoiac Schreber, who found the fixations and detachments of his libido reflected in the fates of the "God-rays" which he invented.[34]

As on a former occasion,[35] we want to avoid the problem as to the origin of the tendency to project psychic processes into the outer world. It is fair to assume, however, that this tendency becomes stronger where the projection into the outer world offers psychic relief. Such a state of affairs can with certainty be expected if the impulses struggling for omnipotence have come into conflict with each other, for then they evidently cannot all become omnipotent. The mor-

[33] We assume that in this early narcistic stage feelings from libidinous and other sources of excitement are perhaps still indistinguishably combined with each other.
[34] Schreber, "Denwürdigkeiten eines Nervenkranken," 1903.— Freud, Psychoanalytic Observations concerning an autobiographically described case of Paranoia, "Jahrbuch für Psychoanalyt. Forsch," Vol. III, 1911.
[35] Compare the latest communication about the Schreber case, p. 59.

bid process in paranoia actually uses the mechanism of projection to solve such conflicts which arise in the psychic life. However, it so happens that the model case of such a conflict between two parts of an antithesis is the ambivalent attitude which we have analyzed in detail in the situation of the mourner at the death of one dear to him. Such a case appeals to us as especially fitted to motivate the creation of projection formations. Here again we are in agreement with those authors who declare that evil spirits were the first born among spirits, and who find the origin of soul conceptions in the impression which death makes upon the survivors. We differ from them only in not putting the intellectual problem which death imposes upon the living into the foreground, instead of which we transfer the force which stimulates inquiry to the conflict of feelings into which this situation plunges the survivor.

The first theoretical accomplishment of man, the creation of spirits, would therefore spring from the same source as the first moral restrictions to which he subjects himself, namely, the rules of taboo. But the fact that they have the same source should not prejudice us in favor of a simultaneous origin. If it really were the situation of the survivor confronted by the dead which first caused primitive man to reflect, so that he was compelled to surrender some of his omnipotence to spirits and to sacrifice a part of the free will of his actions, these cultural creations would be a first recognition of the ἀνάγκη, which opposes man's narcism. Primitive man would bow to the superior power of death with the same gesture with which he seems to deny it.

If we have the courage to follow our assumptions further, we may ask what essential part of our psychological structure is reflected and reviewed in the projection formation of souls and spirits. It is then difficult to dispute that the primitive conception of the soul, though still far removed from the later and wholly immaterial soul, nevertheless shares its nature and therefore looks upon a person or thing as a duality, over the two elements of which the known properties and changes of the whole are distributed. This origin duality, we have borrowed the term from Herbert Spencer,[36] is already identical with the dualism which manifests itself in our customary separation of spirit from body, and whose indestructible linguistic manifestations we recognize, for instance, in the description of a person who faints or raves as one who is "beside himself." [37]

The thing which we, just like primitive man, project into outer reality, can hardly be anything

[36] "Principles of Sociology," Vol. I.
[37] Herbert Spencer, l. c., p. 179.

else than the recognition of a state in which a given thing is present to the senses and to consciousness, next to which another state exists in which the thing is *latent,* but can reappear, that is to say, the co-existence of perception and memory, or, to generalize it, the existence of unconscious psychic processes next to conscious ones.[38] It might be said that in the last analysis the "spirit" of a person or a thing is the faculty of remembering and representing the object, after he or it was withdrawn from conscious perception.

Of course we must not expect from either the primitive or the current conception of the "soul" that its line of demarcation from other parts should be as marked as that which contemporary science draws between conscious and unconscious psychic activity.   The animistic soul, on the contrary, unites determinants from both sides.   Its flightiness and mobility, its faculty of leaving the body, of permanently or temporarily taking possession of another body, all these are characteristics which remind us unmistakably of the nature of consciousness.   But the way in which it keeps itself concealed behind the personal appearance reminds us of the unconscious; to-day

[38] Compare my short paper: "A Note on the Unconscious in Psychoanalysis," in the Proceedings of the Society for Psychical Research, Part LXVI, Vol. XXVI, London, 1912.

we no longer ascribe its unchangeableness and
indestructibility to conscious but to unconscious
processes and look upon these as the real bearers of psychic activity.

We said before that animism is a system of
thought, the first complete theory of the world;
we now want to draw certain inferences through
psychoanalytic interpretation of such a system.
Our everyday experience is capable of constantly
showing us the main characteristics of the "system." We dream during the night and have
learnt to interpret the dream in the daytime.
The dream can, without being untrue to its nature, appear confused and incoherent; but on the
other hand it can also imitate the order of impressions of an experience, infer one occurrence
from another, and refer one part of its content
to another. The dream succeeds more or less
in this, but hardly ever succeeds so completely
that an absurdity or a gap in the structure does
not appear somewhere. If we subject the dream
to interpretation we find that this unstable and
irregular order of its components is quite un-
important for our understanding of it. The essential part of the dream are the dream thoughts,
which have, to be sure, a significant, coherent
order. But their order is quite different from
that which we remember from the manifest content of the dream. The coherence of the dream

thoughts has been abolished and may either remain altogether lost or can be replaced by the
new coherence of the dream content.  Besides
the condensation of the dream elements there is
almost regularly a re-grouping of the same which
is more or less independent of the former order.
We say in conclusion, that what the dream-work
has made out of the material of the dream
thoughts has been subjected to a new influence,
the so-called "secondary elaboration," the object
of which evidently is to do away with the inco-
herence and incomprehensibility caused by the
dream-work, in favor of a new "meaning." This
new meaning which has been brought about by
the secondary elaboration is no longer the meaning of the dream thoughts.

The secondary elaboration of the product of
the dream-work is an excellent example of the
nature and the pretensions of a system.  An intellectual function in us demands the unification,
coherence and comprehensibility of everything
perceived and thought of, and does not hesitate
to construct a false connection if, as a result of
special circumstances, it cannot grasp the right
one. We know such system formations not only
from the dream, but also from phobias, from compulsive thinking and from the types of delusions.
The system formation is most ingenious in delusional states (paranoia) and dominates the

clinical picture, but it also must not be overlooked
in other forms of neuropsychoses. In every case
we can show that a re-arrangement of the psychic
material takes place, which may often be quite
violent, provided it seems comprehensible from
the point of view of the system. The best indication that a system has been formed then lies
in the fact that each result of it can be shown to
have at least two motivations one of which
springs from the assumptions of the system and
is therefore eventually delusional,—and a hidden one which, however, we must recognize as
the real and effective motivation.

An example from a neurosis may serve as il-
lustration. In the chapter on taboo I mentioned
a patient whose compulsive prohibitions correspond very neatly to the taboo of the Maori.[39]
The neurosis of this woman was directed against
her husband and culminated in the defense
against the unconscious wish for his death. But
her manifest systematic phobia concerned the
mention of death in general, in which her husband was altogether eliminated and never became the object of conscious solicitude. One
day she heard her husband give an order to have
his dull razors taken to a certain shop to have
them sharpened. Impelled by a peculiar un-
rest she went to the shop herself and on her re-

turn from this reconnoiter she asked her husband
to lay the razors aside for good because she had
discovered that there was a warehouse of coffins
and funeral accessories next to the shop he mentioned. She claimed that he had intentionally
brought the razors into permanent relation with
the idea of death. This was then the systematic
motivation of the prohibition, but we may be
sure that the patient would have brought home
the prohibition relating to the razors even if she
had not discovered this warehouse in the neigh-
borhood. For it would have been sufficient if on
her way to the shop she had met a hearse, a
person in mourning, or somebody carrying a
wreath. The net of determinants was spread
out far enough to catch the prey in any case, it
was simply a question whether she should pull it
in or not. It could be established with certainty
that she did not mobilize the determinants of the
prohibition in other circumstances. She would
then have said that it had been one of her "better
days." The real reason for the prohibition of
the razor was, of course, as we can easily guess,
her resistance against a pleasurably accentuated
idea that her husband might cut his throat with
the sharpened razors.

In much the same way a motor inhibition, an
abasia or an agoraphobia, becomes perfected and
detailed if the symptom once succeeds in repre-

senting an unconscious wish and of imposing a
defense against it. All the patient's remaining
unconscious phantasies and effective reminiscences strive for symptomatic expression through
this outlet, when once it has been opened, and
range themselves appropriately in the new order
within the sphere of the disturbance of gait. It
would therefore be a futile and really foolish way
to begin to try to understand the symptomatic structure and the details of, let us say, an
agoraphobia, in terms of its basic assumptions.
For the whole logic and strictness of connection
is only apparent. Sharper observation can reveal, as in the formation of the façade in the
dream, the greatest inconsistency and arbitrari-
ness in the symptom formation. The details of
such a systematic phobia take their real motivation from concealed determinants which must
have nothing to do with the inhibition in gait;
it is for this reason that the form of such a phobia
varies so and is so contradictory in different
people.

If we now attempt to retrace the system of
animism with which we are concerned, we may
conclude from our insight into other psychological systems that "superstition" need not be
the only and actual motivation of such a single
rule or custom even among primitive races, and
that we are not relieved of the obligation of seek-

ing for concealed motives. Under the dominance of an animistic system it is absolutely essential that each rule and activity should receive
a systematic motivation which we to-day call
"superstitious." But "superstition," like "anxiety," "dreams," and "demons," is one of the pre-
liminaries of psychology which have been dis-
sipated by psychoanalytic investigation. If we
get behind these structures, which like a screen
conceal understanding, we realize that the psychic
life and the cultural level of savages have hitherto
been inadequately appreciated.

If we regard the repression of impulses as a
measure of the level of culture attained, we must
admit that under the animistic system too, progress and evolution have taken place, which un-
justly have been under-estimated on account of
their superstitious motivation. If we hear that
the warriors of a savage tribe impose the greatest chastity and cleanliness upon themselves as
soon as they go upon the war-path,[40] the obvious
explanation is that they dispose of their refuse
in order that the enemy may not come into possession of this part of their person in order to harm
them by magical means, and we may surmise
analogous superstitious motivations for their ab-
stinence. Nevertheless the fact remains that the
impulse is renounced and we probably under-

[40] Frazer, "Taboo and the Perils of the Soul, p. 158.

stand the case better if we assume that the savage warrior imposes such restrictions upon himself in compensation, because he is on the point of allowing himself the full satisfaction of cruel and hostile impulses otherwise forbidden.  The same holds good for the numerous cases of sexual restriction while he is pre-occupied with difficult or responsible tasks.[41]  Even if the basis of these prohibitions can be referred to some association with magic, the fundamental conception of gaining greater strength by foregoing gratification of desires nevertheless remains unmistakable, and besides the magic rationalization of the prohibition, one must not neglect its hygienic root.  When the men of a savage tribe go away to hunt, fish, make war or collect valuable plants, the women at home are in the meantime subjected to numerous oppressive restrictions which, according to the savages themselves, exert a sympathetic effect upon the success of the far away expedition.  But it does not require much acumen to guess that this element acting at a distance is nothing but a thought of home, the longing of the absent, and that these disguises conceal the sound psychological insight that the men will do their best only if they are fully assured of the whereabouts of their guarded

41 Frazer, l. c., p. 200.

women. On other occasions the thought is directly expressed without magic motivation, that the conjugal infidelity of the wife thwarts the absent husband's efforts.

The countless taboo rules to which the women of savages are subject during their menstrual periods are motivated by the superstitious dread of blood which in all probability actually determines it. But it would be wrong to overlook the possibility that this blood dread also serves æsthetic and hygienic purposes which in every case have to be covered by magic motivations.

We are probably not mistaken in assuming that such attempted explanations expose us to the reproach of attributing a most improbable delicacy of psychic activities to contemporary savages.

But I think that we may easily make the same mistake with the psychology of these races who have remained at the animistic stage that we made with the psychic life of the child, which we adults understood no better and whose richness and fineness of feeling we have therefore so greatly undervalued.

I want to consider another group of hitherto unexplained taboo rules because they admit of an explanation with which the psychoanalyst is familiar. Under certain conditions it is forbid-

den to many savage races to keep in the house
sharp weapons and instruments for cutting.[42]
Frazer cites a German superstition that a knife
must not be left lying with the edge pointing up-
ward because God and the angels might injure
themselves with it.   May we not recognize in this
taboo a premonition of certain "symptomatic
actions "[43] for which the sharp weapon might be
used by unconscious evil impulses?

[42] Frazer, l. c., p. 237.
[43] Freud, "Psychopathology of Everyday Life," p. 215, trans.
by A. A. Brill (The Macmillan Company, N. Y., and T. Fisher
Unwin, London).

# CHAPTER IV

THE reader need not fear that psychoanalysis, which first revealed the regular over-determination of psychic acts and formations, will be tempted to derive anything so complicated as religion from a single source. If it necessarily seeks, as in duty bound, to gain recognition for one of the sources of this institution, it by no means claims exclusiveness for this source or even first rank among the concurring factors. Only a synthesis from various fields of research can decide what relative importance in the genesis of religion is to be assigned to the mechanism which we are to discuss; but such a task exceeds the means as well as the intentions of the psychoanalyst.

## 1

The first chapter of this book made us acquainted with the conception of totemism. We heard that totemism is a system which takes the place of religion among certain primitive races in Australia, America, and Africa, and furnishes the basis of social organization. We know that

in 1869 the Scotchman MacLennan attracted
general interest to the phenomena of totemism,
which until then had been considered merely as
curiosities, by his conjecture that a large number
of customs and usages in various old as well as
modern societies were to be taken as remnants
of a totemic epoch.    Science has since then fully
recognized  this  significance  of  totemism.   I
quote  a  passage  from  the  "Elements  of  the
Psychology of Races" by W. Wundt (1912), as
the latest utterance on this question: [1]   "Taking all this together it becomes highly probable
that a totemic culture was at one time the pre-
liminary stage of every later evolution as well as
a transition stage between the state of primitive
man and the age of gods and heroes."

It is necessary for the purposes of this chapter
to go more deeply into the nature of totemism.
For reasons that will be evident later I here give
preference to an outline by S. Reinach, who in
the year 1900 sketched the following *Code du
totémism* in twelve articles, like a catechism of
the totemic religion: [2]

1.  Certain animals must not be killed or eaten,
but men bring up individual animals of these
species and take care of them.

[1] p. 139.
[2] "Revue Scientifique," October, 1900, reprinted in the four
volume work of the author, "Cultes, Mythes et Religions," 1908,
Tome I, p. 17.

2. An animal that dies accidentally is mourned and buried with the same honors as a member of the tribe.

3. The prohibition as to eating sometimes refers only to a certain part of the animal.

4. If pressure of necessity compels the killing of an animal usually spared, it is done with excuses to the animal and the attempt is made to mitigate the violation of the taboo, namely the killing, through various tricks and evasions.

5. If the animal is sacrificed by ritual, it is solemnly mourned.

6. At specified solemn occasions, like religious ceremonies, the skins of certain animals are donned.   Where totemism still exists, these are totem animals.

7. Tribes and individuals assume the names of totem animals.

8. Many tribes use pictures of animals as coats of arms and decorate their weapons with them; the men paint animal pictures on their bodies or have them tattooed.

9. If the totem is one of the feared and dangerous animals it is assumed that the animal will spare the members of the tribe named after it.

10. The totem animal protects and warns the members of the tribe.

11. The totem animal foretells the future to

those faithful to it and serves as their leader.

12. The members of a totem tribe often believe that they are connected with the totem animal by the bond of common origin.

The value of this catechism of the totem religion can be more appreciated if one bears in mind that Reinach has here also incorporated all the signs and clews which lead to the conclusion that the totemic system had once existed. The peculiar attitude of this author to the problem is shown by the fact that to some extent he neglects the essential traits of totemism, and we shall see that of the two main tenets of the totemistic catechism he has forced one into the background and completely lost sight of the other.

In order to get a more correct picture of the characteristics of totemism we turn to an author who has devoted four volumes to the theme, combining the most complete collection of the observations in question with the most thorough discussion of the problems they raise. We shall remain indebted to J. G. Frazer, the author of "Totemism and Exogamy," [3] for the pleasure and information he affords, even though psychoanalytic investigation may lead us to results which differ widely from his.[4]

3 1910.

4 But it may be well to show the reader beforehand how difficult it is to establish the facts in this field.

"A totem," wrote Frazer in his first essay,[5] "is a class of material objects which a savage regards with superstitious respect, believing that there exists between him and every member of the class an intimate and altogether special relation. The connection between a person and his

In the first place those who collect the observations are not identical with those who digest and discuss them; the first are travelers and missionaries, while the others are scientific men who perhaps have never seen the objects of their research.—It is not easy to establish an understanding with savages. Not all the observers were familiar with the languages but had to use the assistance of interpreters or else had to communicate with the people they questioned in the auxiliary language of pidgin-English. Savages are not communicative about the most intimate affairs of their culture and unburden themselves only to those foreigners who have passed many years in their midst. From various motives they often give wrong or misleading information. (Compare Frazer, "The Beginnings of Religion and Totemism Among the Australian Aborigines," *Fortnightly Review*, 1905, "Totemism and Exogamy," Vol. I, p. 150).—It must not be forgotten that primitive races are not young races but really are as old as the most civilized, and that we have no right to expect that they have preserved their original ideas and institutions for our information without any evolution or distortion. It is certain, on the contrary, that far-reaching changes in all directions have taken place among primitive races, so that we can never unhesitatingly decide which of their present conditions and opinions have preserved the original past, having remained petrified, as it were, and which represent a distortion and change of the original. It is due to this that one meets the many disputes among authors as to what proportion of the peculiarities of a primitive culture is to be taken as a primary, and what as a later and secondary manifestation. To establish the original conditions, therefore, always remains a matter of construction. Finally, it is not easy to adapt oneself to the ways of thinking of primitive races. For like children, we easily misunderstand them, and are always inclined to interpret their acts and feelings according to our own psychic constellations.

[5] "Totemism," Edinburgh, 1887, reprinted in the first volume of his great study, "Totemism and Exogamy."

totem is mutually beneficent; the totem protects the man and the man shows his respect for the totem in various ways, by not killing it if it be an animal, and not cutting or gathering it if it be a plant. As distinguished from a fetich, a totem is never an isolated individual but always a class of objects, generally a species of animals or of plants, more rarely a class of inanimate natural objects, very rarely a class of artificial objects."

At least three kinds of totem can be distinguished:

1. The tribal totem which a whole tribe shares and which is hereditary from generation to generation,

2. The sex totem which belongs to all the masculine or feminine members of a tribe to the exclusion of the opposite sex, and

3. The individual totem which belongs to the individual and does not descend to his successors.

The last two kinds of totem are of comparatively little importance compared to the tribal totem. Unless we are mistaken they are recent formations and of little importance as far as the nature of the taboo is concerned.

The tribal totem (clan totem) is the object of veneration of a group of men and women who take their name from the totem and consider themselves consanguinous offspring of a common ancestor, and who are firmly associated with each other through common obligations towards each other as well as by the belief in their totem.

Totemism is a religious as well as a social system. On its religious side it consists of the relations of mutual respect and consideration between a person and his totem, and on its social side it is composed of obligations of the members of the clan towards each other and towards other tribes. In the later history of totemism these two sides show a tendency to part company; the social system often survives the religious and conversely remnants of totemism remain in the religion of countries in which the social system based upon totemism has disappeared. In the present state of our ignorance about the origin of totemism we cannot say with certainty how these two sides were originally combined. But there is on the whole a strong probability that in the beginning the two sides of totemism were indistinguishable from each other. In other words, the further we go back the clearer it becomes that a member of a tribe looks upon himself as being of the same genus as his totem and makes no distinction between his attitude towards the totem and his attitude towards his tribal companions.

In the special description of totemism as a religious system, Frazer lays stress on the fact that the members of a tribe assume the name of their totem and also as a *rule believe that they are descended from it.* It is due to this belief that they do not hunt the totem animal or kill or eat it, and that they deny themselves every other use of the totem if it is not an animal. The prohibitions against killing or eating the totem are not the only taboos affecting it; sometimes it is also forbidden to touch it and even to look at it; in a number of cases the totem must not be called by its right name. Violation of the taboo prohibitions which protect the totem is punished automatically by serious disease or death.[6]

Specimens of the totem animals are sometimes raised by the clan and taken care of in captivity.[7] A totem animal found dead is mourned and buried like a member of the clan. If a totem animal had to be killed it was done with a prescribed ritual of excuses and ceremonies of expiation.

The tribe expected protection and forbearance from its totem. If it was a dangerous animal, (a beast of prey or a poisonous snake), it was assumed that it would not harm, and where this assumption did not come true the per-

---

[6] Compare the chapter on Taboo.

[7] Just as to-day we still have the wolves in a cage at the steps of the Capitol in Rome and the bears in the pit at Berne.

son attacked was expelled from the tribe. Frazer thinks that oaths were originally ordeals, many tests as to descent and genuineness being in this way left to the decision of the totem. The totem helps in case of illness and gives the tribe premonitions and warnings. The appearance of the totem animal near a house was often looked upon as an announcement of death. The totem had come to get its relative.[8]

A member of a clan seeks to emphasize his relationship to the totem in various significant ways; he imitates an exterior similarity by dressing himself in the skin of the totem animal, by having the picture of it tattooed upon himself, and in other ways. On the solemn occasions of birth, initiation into manhood or funeral obsequies this identification with the totem is carried out in deeds and words. Dances in which all the members of the tribe disguise themselves as their totem and act like it, serve various magic and religious purposes. Finally there are the ceremonies at which the totem animal is killed in a solemn manner.[9]

The social side of totemism is primarily expressed in a sternly observed commandment and in a tremendous restriction. The members of a totem clan are brothers and sisters, pledged to

---

[8] Like the legend of the white woman in many noble families.
[9] l. c., p. 45.—See the discussion of sacrifice further on.

help and protect each other; if a member of the
clan is slain by a stranger the whole tribe of the
slayer must answer for the murder and the clan
of the slain man shows its solidarity in the demand for expiation for the blood that has been
shed. The ties of the totem are stronger than
our ideas of family ties, with which they do not
altogether coincide, since the transfer of the
totem takes place as a rule through maternal
inheritance, paternal inheritance possibly not
counting at all in the beginning.

But the corresponding taboo restriction consists in the prohibition against members of the
same clan marrying each other or having any
kind of sexual intercourse whatsoever with each
other. This is the famous and enigmatic
*exogamy* connection with totemism. We have
devoted the whole first chapter of this book to
it, and therefore need only mention here that
this exogamy springs from the intensified incest
dread of primitive races, that it becomes entirely
comprehensible as a security against incest in
group marriages, and that at first it accomplishes
the avoidance of incest for the younger generation and only in the course of further development becomes a hindrance to the older generation as well.[10]

To this presentation of totemism by Frazer,

[10] See Chapter I.

one of the earliest in the literature on the subject, I will now add a few excerpts from one of
the latest summaries. In the "Elements of the
Psychology of Races" which appeared in 1912,
W. Wundt says:[11] "The totem animal is considered the ancestral animal. 'Totem' is therefore both a group name and a birth name and
in the latter aspect this name has at the same
time a mythological meaning. But all these
uses of the conception play into each other and
the particular meanings may recede so that in
some cases the totems have become almost a
mere nomenclature of the tribal divisions, while
in others the idea of the descent or else the
cultic meaning of the totem remains in the foreground. . . . The conception of the totem determines the *tribal* arrangement and the *tribal*
*organization.* These norms and their establish-
ment in the belief and feelings of the members
of the tribe account for the fact that originally
the totem animal was certainly not considered
merely a name for a group division but that it
usually was considered the progenitor of the corresponding division. . . . This accounted for
the fact that these animal ancestors enjoyed a
cult. . . . This animal cult expresses itself
primarily in the attitude towards the totem animal, quite aside from special ceremonies and

[11] p. 116.

ceremonial festivities: not only each individual
animal but every representative of the same
species was to a certain degree a sanctified animal; the member of the totem was forbidden to
eat the flesh of the totem animal or he was allowed to eat it only under special circumstances.
This is in accord with the significant contradictory phenomenon found in this connection,
namely, that under certain conditions there was
a kind of ceremonial consumption of the totem
flesh. . . ."

". . . But the most important social side of
this totemic tribal arrangement consists in the
fact that it was connected with certain rules of
conduct for the relations of the groups with each
other.  The most important of these were the
rules of conjugal relations.  This tribal division is thus connected with an important phenomenon which first made its appearance in the
totemic age, namely with exogamy."

If we wish to arrive at the characteristics of
the original totemism by sifting through everything that may correspond to later development
or decline, we find the following essential facts:
*The totems were originally only animals and
were considered the ancestors of single tribes.
The totem was hereditary only through the
female  line; it was forbidden to kill the totem
(or to eat it, which under primitive conditions*

amounts to the same thing) ; *members of a totem were forbidden to have sexual intercourse with each other.*[12]

It may now seem strange to us that in the *Code du totémisme* which Reinach has drawn up the one principal taboo, namely exogamy, does not appear at all while the assumption of the second taboo, namely the descent from the totem animal, is only casually mentioned. Yet Reinach is an author to whose work in this field we owe much and I have chosen his presentation in order to prepare us for the differences of opinion among the authors, which will now occupy our attention.

### 2

The more convinced we became that totemism had regularly formed a phase of every culture,

[12] The conclusion which Frazer draws about totemism in his second work on the subject ("The Origin of Totemism," *Fortnight Review*, 1899) agrees with this text: "Thus, totemism has commonly been treated as a primitive system both of religion and of society. As a system of religion it embraces the mystic union of the savage with his totem; as a system of society it comprises the relations in which men and women of the same totem stand to each other and to the members of other totemic groups. And corresponding to these two sides of the system are two rough-and-ready tests or canons of totemism: first, the rule that a man may not kill or eat his totem animal or plant, and second, the rule that he may not marry or cohabit with a woman of the same totem." (p. 101.) Frazer then adds something which takes us into the midst of the discussion about totemism: "Whether the two sides —the religious and the social—have always coexisted or are essentially independent, is a question which has been variously answered."

the more urgent became the necessity of arriving at an understanding of it and of casting light upon the riddle of its nature. To be sure, everything about totemism is in the nature of a riddle; the decisive questions are the origin of the totem, , the motivation of exogamy (or rather of the incest taboo which it represents) and the relation between the two, the totem organization and the incest prohibition. The understanding should be at once historical and psychological; it should inform us under what conditions this peculiar institution developed and to what psychic needs of man it has given expression.

The reader will certainly be astonished to hear from how many different points of view the answer to these questions has been attempted and how far the opinions of expert investigators vary. Almost everything that might be asserted in general about totemism is doubtful; even the above statement of it, taken from an article by Frazer in 1887, cannot escape the criticism that it expresses an arbitrary preference of the author and would be challenged to-day by Frazer himself, who has repeatedly changed his view on the subject.[13]

[13] In connection with such a change of opinion Frazer made this excellent statement: "That my conclusions on these difficult questions are final, I am not so foolish as to pretend. I have changed my views repeatedly, and I am resolved to change them again with every change of the evidence, for like a chameleon the enquirer

It is quite obvious that the nature of totemism and exogamy could be most readily grasped if we could get into closer touch with the origin of both institutions.  But in judging the state of affairs we must not forget the remark of Andrew Lang, that even primitive races have not pre-served these original forms and the conditions of their origin, so that we are altogether depend-ent upon hypotheses to take the place of the observation we lack.[14]  Among the attempted explanations some seem inadequate from the very beginning in the judgment of the psycholo-gist.  They are altogether too rational and do not take into consideration the effective character of what they are to explain.  Others rest on assumptions which observation fails to verify; while still others appeal to facts which could bet-ter be subjected to another interpretation.  The refutation of these various opinions as a rule hardly presents any difficulties; the authors are, as usual, stronger in the criticism which they practice on each other than in their own work. The final result as regards most of the points treated is a *non liquet*.  It is therefore not sur-

should shift his colours with the shifting colours of the ground he treads."   Preface to Vol. I, "Totemism and Exogamy," 1910.

[14] "By the nature of the case, as the origin of totemism lies far beyond our powers of historical examination or of experiment, we must have recourse as regards this matter, to conjecture," Andrew Lang, "Secret of the Totem," p. 27.—"Nowhere do we see abso-lutely primitive man, and a totemic system in the making," p. 29.

prising that most of the new literature on the subject, which we have largely omitted here, shows the unmistakable effort to reject a general solution of totemic problems as unfeasible. (See, for instance, B. Goldenweiser in the Journal of American Folklore XXIII, 1910. Reviewed in the Britannica Year Book 1913.) I have taken the liberty of disregarding the chronological order in stating these contradictory hypotheses.

### a) THE ORIGIN OF TOTEMISM

The question of the origin of totemism can also be formulated as follows:   How did primitive people come to select the names of animals, plants and inanimate objects for themselves and their tribes? [15]

The Scotchman, MacLennan, who discovered totemism and exogamy for science,[16] refrained from publishing his views of the origin of totemism.   According to a communication of Andrew Lang [17] he was for a time inclined to trace totemism back to the custom of tattooing.   I shall divide the accepted theories of the derivation of

---

[15] At first probably only animals.

[16] "The Worship of Animals and Plants," *Fortnightly Review,* 1869–1870.  "Primitive Marriage," 1865; both works reprinted in "Studies in Ancient History," 1876; second edition, 1886.

[17] "The Secret of the Totem," 1905, p. 34.

totemism into three groups, α) nominalistic, β) sociological, γ) psychological.

## α) *The Nominalistic Theories*

The information about these theories will justify their summation under the headings I have used.

Garcilaso de La Vega, a descendant of the Peruvian Inkas, who wrote the history of his race in the seventeenth century is already said to have traced back what was known to him about totemic phenomena to the need of the tribes to differentiate themselves from each other by means of names.[18] The same idea appears centuries later in the "Ethnology" of A. K. Keane where totems are said to be derived from heraldic badges through which individuals, families and tribes wanted to differentiate themselves.[19]

Max Müller expresses the same opinion about the meaning of the totem in his "Contributions to the Science of Mythology."[20] A totem is said to be, 1. a mark of the clan, 2. a clan name, 3. the name of the ancestor of the clan, 4. the name of the object which the clan reveres. J. Pikler wrote later, in 1899, that men needed a perma-

18 Ibid.
19 Ibid.
20 According to Andrew Lang.

nent name for communities and individuals that
could be preserved in writing. . . . Thus totemism arises, not from a religious, but from a pro-
saic everyday need of mankind. The giving of
names, which is the essence of totemism, is a
result of the technique of primitive writing.
The totem is of the nature of an easily represented writing symbol. But if savages first bore
the name of an animal they deduced the idea of
relationship from this animal.[21]

Herbert Spencer,[22] also, thought that the
origin of totemism was to be found in the giving
of names. The attributes of certain individuals,
he showed, had brought about their being named
after animals so that they had come to have
names of honor or nicknames which continued in
their descendants. As a result of the indefiniteness and incomprehensibility of primitive
languages, these names are said to have been
taken by later generations as proof of their descent from the animals themselves. Totemism
would thus be the result of a mistaken reverence
for ancestors.

Lord Avebury (better known under his former name, Sir John Lubbock) has expressed

[21] Pikler and Somló, "The Origin of Totemism," 1901. The authors rightly call their attempt at explanation a "Contribution to
the materialistic theory of History."

[22] "The Origin of Animal Worship," *Fortnightly Review*, 1870.
"Principles of Psychology," Vol. I, paragraphs 169 to 176.

himself quite similarly about the origin of totemism, though without emphasizing the misunderstanding. If we want to explain the veneration of animals we must not forget how often human names are borrowed from animals. The children and followers of a man who was called bear or lion naturally made this their ancestral name. In this way it came about that the animal itself came to be respected and finally venerated.

Fison has advanced what seems an irrefutable objection to such a derivation of the totem name from the names of individuals.[23] He shows from conditions in Australia that the totem is always the mark of a group of people and never of an individual. But if it were otherwise, if the totem was originally the name of a single individual, it could never, with the system of maternal inheritance, descend to his children.

The theories thus far stated are evidently inadequate. They may explain how animal names came to be applied to primitive tribes but they can never explain the importance attached to the giving of names which constitutes the totemic system. The most noteworthy theory of this group has been developed by Andrew Lang in his books, Social Origins, 1903, and The

[23] Kamilaroi and Kurmai, p. 165, 1880 (Lang, "Secret of the Totem," etc.).

Secret of the Totem, 1905. This theory still makes naming the center of the problem, but it uses two interesting psychological factors and thus may claim to have contributed to the final solution of the riddle of totemism.

Andrew Lang holds that it does not make any difference how clans acquired their animal names. It might be assumed that one day they awoke to the consciousness that they had them without being able to account from where they came. *The origin of these names had been forgotten.* In that case they would seek to acquire more information by pondering over their names, and with their conviction of the importance of names they necessarily came to all the ideas that are contained in the totemic system. For primitive men, as for savages of to-day and even for our children,[24] a name is not indifferent and conventional as it seems to us, but is something important and essential. A man's name is one of the main constituents of his person and perhaps a part of his psyche. The fact that they had the same names as animals must have led primitive men to assume a secret and important bond between their persons and the particular animal species. What other bond than consanguinity could it be? But if the similarity of names once led to this assumption it could also account di-

[24] See the chapter on Taboo, p. 95.

rectly for all the totemic prohibitions of the blood taboo, including exogamy.

"No more than these three things—a group animal name of unknown origin; belief in a transcendental connection between all bearers, human and bestial, of the same name; and belief in the blood superstitions—were needed to give rise to all the totemic creeds and practices, including exogamy," (Secret of The Totem, p. 126.)

Lang's explanation extends over two periods. It derives the totemic system of psychological necessity from the totem names, on the assumption that the origin of the naming has been forgotten. The other part of the theory now seeks to clear up the origin of these names. We shall see that it bears an entirely different stamp.

This other part of the Lang theory is not markedly different from those which I have called "nominalistic." The practical need of differentiation compelled the individual tribes to assume names and therefore they tolerated the names which every tribe ascribed to the other. This "naming from without" is the peculiarity of Lang's construction. The fact that the names which thus originated were borrowed from animals is not further remarkable and need not have been felt by primitive men as abuse or derision. Besides, Lang has cited numerous cases from later epochs of history in which names given from without that were first meant to be derisive were accepted by those nicknamed and voluntarily born, (The Guises, Whigs and Tories). The assumption that the origin of these names was forgotten in the course of time connects this second part of the Lang theory with the first one just mentioned.

### β) *The Sociological Theories*

S. Reinach, who successfully traced the relics of the totemic system in the cult and customs of later periods, though attaching from the very beginning only slight value to the factor of descent from the totem animal, once made the casual remark that totemism seemed to him to be nothing but *"une hypertrophie de l'instinct social."* [25]

The same interpretation seems to permeate the new work of E. Durkheim, Les formes élémentaires de la vie religieuse; Le système totémique en Australie, 1912. The totem is the visible representative of the social religion of these races. It embodies the community, which is the real object of veneration.

Other authors have sought a more intimate reason for the share which social impulses have played in the formation of totemic institutions.

[25] l. c., Vol. I, p. 41.

Thus A. C. Haddon has assumed that every primitive tribe originally lived on a particular plant or animal species and perhaps also traded with this food and exchanged it with other tribes. It then was inevitable that a tribe should become known to other tribes by the name of the animal which played such weighty rôle with it. At the same time this tribe would develop a special familiarity with this animal, and a kind of interest for it which, however, was based upon the psychic motive of man's most elementary and pressing need, namely, hunger.[26]

The objections against this most rational of all the totem theories are that such a state of the food supply is never found among primitive men and probably never existed. Savages are the more omnivorous the lower they stand in the social scale. Besides, it is incomprehensible how such an exclusive diet could have developed an almost religious relation to the totem, culminating in an absolute abstention from the preferred food.

The first of the three theories about the origin of totemism which Frazer stated was a psychological one. We shall report it elsewhere.

Frazer's second theory, which we will discuss here, originated under the influence of an im-

[26] Address to the Anthropological Section, British Association, Belfast, 1902. According to Frazer, l. c., Vol. IV, p. 50.

portant publication by two investigators of the inhabitants of Central Australia.[27]

Spencer and Gillen describe a series of peculiar institutions, customs, and opinions of a group of tribes, the so-called Arunta nation, and Frazer subscribes to their opinion that these peculiarities are to be looked upon as characteristics of a primary state and that they can explain the first and real meaning of totemism.

In the Arunta tribe itself (a part of the Arunta nation) these peculiarities are as follows:

1. They have the division into totem clans but the totem is not hereditary but is individually determined (as will be shown later).

2. The totem clans are not exogamous, and the marriage restrictions are brought about by a highly developed division into marriage classes which have nothing to do with the totems.

3. The function of the totem clan consists of carrying out a ceremony which in a subtle magic manner brings about an increase of the edible totem. (This ceremony is called *Intichiuma*.)

4. The Aruntas have a peculiar theory about conception and re-birth. They assume that the spirits of the dead who belonged to their totem wait for their re-birth in definite localities and

[27] "The Native Tribes of Central Australia" by Baldwin Spencer and H. J. Gillen, London, 1891.

penetrate into the bodies of the women who pass such a spot. When a child is born the mother states at which spirit abode she thinks she conceived her child. This determines the totem of the child. It is further assumed that the spirits (of the dead as well as of the re-born) are bound to peculiar stone amulets, called *Churinga*, which are found in these places.

Two factors seem to have induced Frazer to believe that the oldest form of totemism had been found in the institution of the Aruntas. In the first place the existence of certain myths which assert that the ancestors of the Aruntas always lived on their totem animal, and that they married no other women except those of their own totem. Secondly, the apparent disregard of the sexual act in their theory of conception. People who had not yet realized that conception was the result of the sexual act might well be considered the most backward and primitive people living to-day.

Frazer, in having recourse to the *Intichiuma* ceremony to explain totemism, suddenly saw the totemic system in a totally different light as a thoroughly practical organization for accomplishing the most natural needs of man. (Compare Haddon above.[28]) The system was simply

[28] There is nothing vague or mystical about it, nothing of that metaphysical haze which some writers love to conjure up over the

an extraordinary piece of "coöperative magic."
Primitive men formed what might be called a
magic production and consumption club. Each
totem clan undertook to see to the cleanliness of
a certain article of food. If it were a question of
inedible totems like harmful animals, rain, wind,
or similar objects, it was the duty of the totem
clan to dominate this part of nature and to ward
off its injuriousness. The efforts of each clan
were for the good of all the others. As the clan
could not eat its totem or could eat only a very
little of it, it furnished this valuable product for
the rest and was in turn furnished with what
these had to take care of as their social totem
duty. In the light of this interpretation furnished by the *Intichiuma* ceremony, it appeared
to Frazer as if the prohibition against eating the
totem had misled observers to neglect the more
important side of the relation, namely the commandment to supply as much as possible of the
edible totem for the needs of others.

Frazer accepted the tradition of the Aruntas
that each totem clan had originally lived on its
totem without any restriction. It then became
difficult to understand the evolution that followed through which savages were satisfied to

humblest beginnings of human speculation but which is utterly
foreign to the simple, sensuous, and concrete modes of the savage.
("Totemism and Exogamy," I., p. 117.)

insure the totem for others while they themselves
abstained from eating it.   He then assumed that
this restriction was by no means the result of a
kind of religious respect, but came about through
the observation that no animal devoured its own
kind, so that this break in the identification with
the totem was injurious to the power which
savages sought to acquire over the totem.   Or
else it resulted from the endeavor to make the
being favorably disposed by sparing it.   Frazer
did not conceal the difficulties of this explanation from himself,[29] nor did he dare to indicate
in what way the habit of marrying within the
totem, which the myths of the Aruntas pro-
claimed, was converted into exogamy.

Frazer's theory based on the *Intichiuma,*
stands and falls with the recognition of the
primitive nature of the Arunta institutions.
But it seems impossible to hold to this in the fact
of the objections advanced by Durkheim [30] and
Lang.[31]   The Aruntas seem on the contrary to
be the most developed of the Australian tribes
and to represent rather a dissolution stage of
totemism than its beginning.   The myths that
made such an impression on Frazer because they
emphasize, in contrast to prevailing institutions

[29] l. c., p. 120.
[30] "L'année Sociologique," Vol. I, V, VIII, and elsewhere.   See
especially the chapter, "Sur le Totemisme," Vol. V, 1901.
[31] "Social Origins and the Secret of the Totem."

of to-day, that the Aruntas are free to eat the totem and to marry within it, easily explain themselves to us as wish phantasies which are projected into the past, like the myths of the Golden Age.

### γ) *The Psychological Theories*

Frazer's first psychological theories, formed before his acquaintance with the observations of Spencer and Gillen, were based upon the belief in an "outward soul." [32] The totem was meant to represent a safe place of refuge where the soul is deposited in order to avoid the dangers which threaten it. After primitive man had housed his soul in his totem he himself became invulnerable and he naturally took care himself not to harm the bearer of his soul. But as he did not know which individual of the species in question was the bearer of his soul he was concerned in sparing the whole species. Frazer himself later gave up this derivation of totemism from the belief in souls.

When he became acquainted with the observations of Spencer and Gillen he set up the other social theory which has just been stated, but he himself then saw that the motive from which he had derived totemism was altogether too "rational" and that he had assumed a social organi-

[32] "The Golden Bough," II, p. 332.

zation for it which was altogether too complicated to be called primitive.[33] The magic coöperative companies now appeared to him rather as the fruit than as the germ of totemism. He sought a simpler factor for the derivation of totemism in the shape of a primitive superstition behind these forms. He then found this original factor in the remarkable conception theory of the Aruntas.

As already stated, the Aruntas establish no connection between conception and the sexual act. If a woman feels herself to be a mother it means that at that moment one of the spirits from the nearest spirit abode who has been watching for a re-birth, has penetrated into her body and is born as her child. This child has the same totem as all the spirits that lurk in that particular locality. But if we are willing to go back a step further and assume that the woman originally believed that the animal, plant, stone or other object which occupied her fancy at the moment when she first felt herself pregnant had really penetrated into her and was being born through her in human form, then the identity of a human being with his totem would really

[33] "It is unlikely that a community of savages should deliberately parcel out the realm of nature into provinces, assign each province to a particular band of magicians, and bid all the bands to work their magic and weave their spells for the common good." "Totemism and Exogamy," Vol. IV, p. 57,

be founded on the belief of the mother, and all the other totem commandments (with the exception of exogamy) could easily be derived from this belief. Men would refuse to eat the particular animal or plant because it would be just like eating themselves. But occasionally they would be impelled to eat some of their totem in a ceremonial manner because they could thus strengthen their identification with the totem, which is the essential part of totemism. W. H. R. Rivers' observations among the inhabitants of the Bank Islands seemed to prove men's direct identification with their totems on the basis of such a conception theory.[34]

The ultimate sources of totemism would then be the ignorance of savages as to the process of procreation among human beings and animals; especially their ignorance as to the rôle which the male plays in fertilization. This ignorance must be facilitated by the long interval which is interposed between the fertilizing act and the birth of the child or the sensation of the child's first movements. Totemism is therefore a creation of the feminine mind and not of the masculine. The sick fancies of the pregnant woman are the roots of it. "Anything indeed that struck a woman at that mysterious moment of her life when she first knows herself to be a

[34] "Totemism and Exogamy," II, p. 89, and IV, p. 59.

mother might easily be identified by her with the child in her womb. Such maternal fancies, so natural and seemingly so universal, appear to be the root of totemism.[35]

The main objection to this third theory of Frazer's is the same which has already been advanced against his second, sociological theory. The Aruntas seem to be far removed from the beginnings of totemism: Their denial of fatherhood does not apparently rest upon primitive ignorance; in many cases they even have paternal inheritance. They seem to have sacrificed fatherhood to a kind of a speculation which strives to honor the ancestral spirits.[36] Though they raise the myth of immaculate conception through a spirit to a general theory of conception, we cannot for that reason credit them with ignorance as to the conditions of procreation any more than we could the old races who lived during the rise of the Christian myths.

Another psychological theory of the origin of totemism has been formulated by the Dutch writer, G. A. Wilcken. It establishes a connection between totemism and the migration of souls. "The animal into which, according to general belief, the souls of the dead passed, be-

---

[35] "Totemism and Exogamy," IV, p. 63.

[36] "That belief is a philosophy far from primitive," Andrew Lang, "Secret of the Totem," p. 192.

came a blood relative, an ancestor, and was
revered as such." But the belief in the soul's
migration to animals is more readily derived
from totemism than inversely.[37]

Still another theory of totemism is advanced
by the excellent American ethnologists, Franz
Boas, Hill-Tout, and others. It is based on
observations of totemic Indian tribes and asserts
that the totem is originally the guardian spirit of
an ancestor who has acquired it through a dream
and handed it on to his descendants. We have
already heard the difficulties which the derivation
of totemism through inheritance from a single
individual offers; besides, the Australian observations seem by no means to support the tracing
back of the totem to the guardian spirit.[38]

Two facts have become decisive for the last of
the psychological theories as stated by Wundt;
in the first place, that the original and most
widely known totem object was an animal,
and secondly, that the earliest totem animals
corresponded to animals which had a soul.[39]
Such animals as birds, snakes, lizards, mice
are fitted by their extreme mobility, their
flight through the air, and by other characteristics which arouse surprise and fear, to become

---

[37] Frazer, "Totemism and Exogamy," IV, p. 45.
[38] Frazer, l. c., p. 48.
[39] Wundt, "Elemente der Völker Psychologie," p. 190.

the bearers of souls which leave their bodies. The totem animal is a descendant of the animal transformations of the spirit-soul. Thus with Wundt totemism is directly connected with the belief in souls or with animism.

b) and c) *The Origin of Exogamy and Its Relation to Totemism*

I have put forth the theories of totemism with considerable detail and yet I am afraid that I have not made them clear enough on account of the condensation that was constantly necessary. In the interest of the reader I am taking the liberty of further condensing the other questions that arise. The discussions about the exogamy of totem races become especially complicated and untractable, one might even say confused, on account of the nature of the material used. Fortunately the object of this treatise permits me to limit myself to pointing out several guide-posts and referring to the frequently quoted writings of experts in the field for a more thorough pursuit of the subject.

The attitude of an author to the problems of exogamy is of course not independent of the stand he has taken toward one or the other of the totem theories. Some of these explanations of totemism lack all connection with exogamy so that the two institutions are entirely separated. Thus we find here two opposing views, one of which clings to the original likelihood that exogamy is an essential part of the totemic system while the other disputes such a connection and believes in an accidental combination of these two traits of the most ancient cultures. In his later works Frazer has emphatically stood for this latter point of view.

"I must request the reader to bear constantly in mind that the two institutions of totemism and exogamy are fundamentally distinct in origin and nature though they have accidentally crossed and blended in many tribes." (Totemism and Exogamy I, Preface XII.)

He warns directly against the opposite view as being a source of endless difficulties and misunderstandings. In contrast to this, many authors have found a way of conceiving exogamy as a necessary consequence of the basic views on totemism. Durkheim [40] has shown in his writings how the taboo, which is attached to the totem, must have entailed the prohibition against putting a woman of the same totem to sexual uses. The totem is of the same blood as the human being and for this reason the blood bann (in reference to defloration and menstruation) forbids sexual intercourse with a woman of the

[40] "L'année Sociologique," 1898–1904.

same totem.[41]   Andrew Lang, who here agrees
with Durkheim, goes so far as to believe that the
blood taboo was not necessary to bring about the
prohibition in regard to the women of the same
tribe.[42]   The general totem taboo which, for instance, forbids any one to sit in the shadow of the
totem tree, would have sufficed.   Andrew Lang
also contends for another derivation of exogamy
(see below) and leaves it in doubt how these two
explanations are related to each other.

As regards the temporal relations, the majority of authors subscribe to the opinion that
totemism is the older institution and that exogamy came later.[43]

Among the theories which seek to explain
exogamy independently of totemism only a few
need be mentioned in so far as they illustrate
different attitudes of the authors towards the
problem of incest.

MacLennan [44] had ingeniously guessed that
exogamy resulted from the remnants of customs
pointing to earlier forms of female rape.   He
assumed that it was the general custom in an-

---

[41] See Frazer's "Criticism of Durkheim, Totemism and Exogamy," p. 101.

[42] "Secret," etc., p. 125.

[43] See Frazer, l. c. IV, p. 75: "The totemic clan is a totally
different social organism from the exogamous class, and we have
good grounds for thinking that it is far older."

[44] "Primitive Marriage," 1865.

cient times to procure women from strange
tribes so that marriage with a woman from the
same tribe gradually became "improper because
it was unusual." He sought the motive for the
exogamous habit in the scarcity of women among
these tribes, which had resulted from the custom
of killing most female children at birth. We
are not concerned here with investigating
whether actual conditions corroborate MacLennan's assumptions. We are more interested in
the argument that these premises still leave it
unexplained why the male members of the tribe
should have made these few women of their blood
inaccessible to themselves, as well as in the manner in which the incest problem is here entirely
neglected.[45]

Other writers have on the contrary assumed,
and evidently with more right, that exogamy is
to be interpreted as an institution for the prevention of incest.[46]

If we survey the gradually increasing complication of Australian marriage restrictions we
can hardly help agreeing with the opinion of
Morgan, Frazer, Hewitt and Baldwin Spencer,[47]
that these institutions bear the stamp of "deliber-
ate design," as Frazer puts it, and that they were

[45] Frazer, l. c., p. 73 to 92.
[46] Compare Chapter I.
[47] Morgan, "Ancient Society," 1877.—Frazer, "Totemism and
Exogamy," IV, p. 105.

meant to do what they have actually accomplished. "In no other way does it seem possible to explain in all its details a system at once so complex and so regular." [48]

It is of interest to point out that the first restrictions which the introduction of marriage classes brought about affected the sexual freedom of the younger generation, in other words, incest between brothers and sisters and between sons and mothers, while incest between father and daughter was only abrogated by more sweeping measures.

However, to trace back exogamous sexual restrictions to legal intentions does not add anything to the understanding of the motive which created these institutions. From what source, in the final analysis, springs the dread of incest which must be recognized as the root of exogamy? It evidently does not suffice to appeal to an instinctive aversion against sexual intercourse with blood relatives, that is to say, to the fact of incest dread, in order to explain the dread of incest, if social experience shows that, in spite of this instinct, incest is not a rare occurrence even in our society, and if the experience of history can acquaint us with cases in which incestuous marriage of privileged persons was made the rule.

[48] Frazer, l. c., p. 106.

Westermarck [49] advanced the following to explain the dread of incest: "that an innate aversion against sexual intercourse exists between persons who live together from childhood and that this feeling, since such persons are as a rule consanguinous, finds a natural expression in custom and law through the abhorrence of sexual intercourse between those closely related." Though Havelock Ellis disputed the instinctive character of this aversion in his "Studies in the Psychology of Sex," he otherwise supported the same explanation in its essentials by declaring: "The normal absence of the manifestation of the pairing instinct where brothers and sisters or boys and girls living together from childhood are concerned, is a purely negative phenomenon due to the fact that under these circumstances the antecedent conditions for arousing the mating instinct must be entirely lacking. . . . For persons who have grown up together from childhood habit has dulled the sensual attraction of seeing, hearing and touching and has led it into a channel of quiet attachment, robbing it of its power to call forth the necessary erethistic excitement required to produce sexual tumescence."

[49] "Origin and Development of Moral Conceptions," Vol. II, "Marriage," 1909. See also there the author's defense against familiar objections.

It seems to me very remarkable that Westermarck looks upon this innate aversion to sexual intercourse with persons with whom we have shared childhood as being at the same time a psychic representative of the biological fact that inbreeding means injury to the species. Such a biological instinct would hardly go so far astray in its psychological manifestation as to affect the companions of home and hearth which in this respect are quite harmless, instead of the blood relatives which alone are injurious to procreation. And I cannot resist citing the excellent criticism which Frazer opposes to Westermarck's assertion. Frazer finds it incomprehensible that sexual sensibility to-day is not at all opposed to sexual intercourse with companions of the hearth and home while the dread of incest, which is said to be nothing but an offshoot of this reluctance, has nowadays grown to be so overpowering. But other remarks of Frazer's go deeper and I set them down here in unabbreviated form because they are in essential agreement with the arguments developed in my chapter on taboo.

"It is not easy to see why any deep human instinct should need reinforcement through law. There is no law commanding men to eat and drink, or forbidding them to put their hands in the fire. Men eat and drink and keep their hands out of the fire instinctively, for fear of natural, not legal penalties, which would be entailed by violence done to these instincts. The law only forbids men to do what their instincts incline them to do; what nature itself prohibits and punishes it would be superfluous for the law to prohibit and punish. Accordingly we may always safely assume that crimes forbidden by law are crimes which many men have a natural propensity to commit. If there were no such propensity there would be no such crimes, and if no such crimes were committed, what need to forbid them? Instead of assuming therefore, from the legal prohibition of incest, that there is a natural aversion to incest we ought rather to assume that there is a natural instinct in favor of it, and that if the law represses it, it does so because civilized men have come to the conclusion that the satisfaction of these natural instincts is detrimental to the general interests of society." [50]

To this valuable argument of Frazer's I can add that the experiences of psychoanalysis make the assumption of such an innate aversion to incestuous relations altogether impossible. They have taught, on the contrary, that the first sexual impulses of the young are regularly of an incestuous nature and that such repressed impulses

[50] l. c., p. 97,

play a rôle which can hardly be overestimated as the motive power of later neuroses.

The interpretation of incest dread as an innate instinct must therefore be abandoned. The same holds true of another derivation of the incest prohibition which counts many supporters, namely, the assumption that primitive races very soon observed the dangers with which inbreeding threatened their race and that they therefore had decreed the incest prohibition with a conscious purpose. The objections to this attempted explanation crowd upon each other.[51] Not only must the prohibition of incest be older than all breeding of domestic animals from which men could derive experience of the effect of inbreeding upon the characteristics of the breed, but the harmful consequences of inbreeding are not established beyond all doubt even to-day and in man they can be shown only with difficulty. Besides, everything that we know about contemporaneous savages makes it very improbable that the thoughts of their far-removed ancestors should already have been occupied with preventing injury to their later descendants. It sounds almost ridiculous to attribute hygienic and eugenic motives such as have hardly yet found consideration in our culture, to these

[51] Compare Durkheim, "La prohibition de l'inceste." "L'année Sociologique,' I, 1896–97.

children of the race who lived without thought of the morrow.[52]

And finally it must be pointed out that a prohibition against inbreeding as an element weakening to the race, which is imposed from practical hygienic motives, seems quite inadequate to explain the deep abhorrence which our society feels against incest. This dread of incest, as I have shown elsewhere,[53] seems to be even more active and stronger among primitive races living to-day than among the civilized.

In inquiring into the origin of incest dread it could be expected that here also there is the choice between possible explanations of a sociological, biological, and psychological nature in which the psychological motives might have to be considered as representative of biological forces. Still, in the end, one is compelled to subscribe to Frazer's resigned statement, namely, that we do not know the origin of incest dread and do not even know how to guess at it. None of the solutions of the riddle thus far advanced seems satisfactory to us.[54]

I must mention another attempt to explain the

[52] Charles Darwin says about savages: "They are not likely to reflect on distant evils to their progeny."

[53] See Chapter I.

[54] "Thus the ultimate origin of exogamy and with it the law of incest—since exogamy was devised to prevent incest—remains a problem nearly as dark as ever." "Totemism and Exogamy," I, p. 165.

origin of incest dread which is of an entirely
different nature from those considered up to
now. It might be called a historic explanation.

This attempt is associated with a hypothesis
of Charles Darwin about the primal social state
of man. From the habits of the higher apes
Darwin concluded that man, too, lived originally
in small hordes in which the jealousy of the oldest and strongest male prevented sexual promis-
cuity. "We may indeed conclude from what we
know of the jealousy of all male quadrupeds,
armed, as many of them are, with special weapons for battling with their rivals, that promis-
cuous intercourse in a state of nature is extremely
improbable. . . . If we therefore look back
far enough into the stream of time and judging
from the social habits of man as he now exists,
the most probable view is that he originally lived
in small communities, each with a single wife, or
if powerful with several, whom he jealously de-
fended against all other men. Or he may not
have been a social animal and yet have lived with
several wives, like the gorilla; for all the natives
"agree that only the adult male is seen in a band;
when the young male grows up a contest takes
place for mastery, and the strongest, by killing
and driving out the others, establishes himself
as the head of the community (Dr. Savage in
the Boston Journal of Natural History, Vol.

V, 1845-47). The younger males being thus
driven out and wandering about would also, when
at last successful in finding a partner, prevent too
close inbreeding within the limits of the same
family." [55]

Atkinson [56] seems to have been the first to recognize that these conditions of the Darwinian
primal horde would in practice bring about the
exogamy of the young men. Each one of those
driven away could found a similar horde in
which, thanks to jealousy of the chief, the same
prohibition as to sexual intercourse obtained, and
in the course of time these conditions would have
brought about the rule which is now known as
law: no sexual intercourse with the members
of the horde. After the advent of totemism the
rule would have changed into a different form:
no sexual intercourse within the totem.

Andrew Lang [57] declared himself in agreement with this explanation of exogamy. But
in the same book he advocates the other theory of
Durkheim which explains exogamy as a consequence of the totem laws. It is not altogether
easy to combine the two interpretations; in the
first case exogamy would have existed before

[55] "The Origin of Man," Vol. II, Chapter 20, pp. 603-604.
[56] "Primal Law," London, 1903 (with Andrew Lang, "Social
Origins").
[57] "Secret of the Totem, pp. 114, 143.

totemism; in the second case it would be a consequence of it.[58]

### 3

Into this darkness psychoanalytic experience throws one single ray of light.

The relation of the child to animals has much in common with that of primitive man. The child does not yet show any trace of the pride which afterwards moves the adult civilized man to set a sharp dividing line between his own nature and that of all other animals. The child unhesitatingly attributes full equality to animals; he probably feels himself more closely related to the animal than to the undoubtedly mysterious adult, in the freedom with which he acknowledges his needs.

[58] "If it be granted that exogamy existed in practice, on the lines of Mr. Darwin's theory, before the totem beliefs lent to the practice a *sacred* sanction, our task is relatively easy. The first practical rule would be that of the jealous sire: "No males to touch the females in my camp," with expulsion of adolescent sons. *In efflux of time that rule, become habitual*, would be, "No marriages within the local group." Next let the local groups receive names such as Emus, Crows, Opossums, Snipes, and the rule becomes, "No marriage within the local group of animal name; no Snipe to marry a Snipe." But, if the primal groups were not exogamous they would become so as soon as totemic myths and taboos were developed out of the animal, vegetable, and other names of small local groups." "Secret of the Totem," p. 143. (The italics above are mine).—In his last expression on the subject, ("Folklore," December, 1911) Andrew Lang states, however, that he has given up the derivation of exogamy out of the "general totemic" taboo.

Not infrequently a curious disturbance manifests itself in this excellent understanding between child and animal. The child suddenly
begins to fear a certain animal species and to
protect himself against seeing or touching any individual of this species. There results the clinical picture of an *animal phobia,* which is one of
the most frequent among the psychoneurotic diseases of this age and perhaps the earliest form
of such an ailment. The phobia is as a rule in
regard to animals for which the child has until
then shown the liveliest interest and has nothing
to do with the individual animal. In cities the
choice of animals which can become the object
of phobia is not great. They are horses, dogs,
cats, more seldom birds, and strikingly often
very small animals like bugs and butterflies.
Sometimes animals which are known to the child
only from picture books and fairy stories become
objects of the senseless and inordinate anxiety
which is manifested with these phobias; it is seldom possible to learn the manner in which such
an unusual choice of anxiety has been brought
about. I am indebted to Dr. Karl Abraham
for the report of a case in which the child itself
explained its fear of wasps by saying that the
color and the stripes of the body of the wasp had
made it think of the tiger of which, from all that
it had heard, it might well be afraid.

The animal phobias have not yet been made the object of careful analytical investigation, although they very much merit it. The difficulties of analyzing children of so tender an age have probably been the motive of such neglect. It cannot therefore be asserted that the general meaning of these illnesses is known, and I myself do not think that it would turn out to be the same in all cases. But a number of such phobias directed against larger animals have proved accessible to analysis and have thus betrayed their secret to the investigator. In every case it was the same: the fear at bottom was of the father, if the children examined were boys, and was merely displaced upon the animal.

Every one of any experience in psychoanalysis has undoubtedly seen such cases and has received the same impression from them. But I can refer to only a few detailed reports on the subject. This is an accident of the literature of such cases, from which the conclusion should not be drawn that our general assertion is based on merely scattered observation. For instance I mention an author, M. Wulff of Odessa, who has very intelligently occupied himself with the neuroses of childhood. He tells, in relating the history of an illness, that a nine year old boy suffered from a dog phobia at the age of four. "When he saw a dog running by on the street he wept and cried:

'Dear dog, don't touch me, I will be good.'"
By "being good" he meant "not to play violin
any more" (to practice onanism).[58a]

The same author later sums up as follows:
"His dog phobia is really his fear of the father
displaced upon the dog, for his peculiar expression: 'Dog, I will be good'—that is to say, I will
not masturbate—really refers to the father, who
has forbidden masturbation." He then adds
something in a note which fully agrees with my
experience and at the same time bears witness to
the abundance of such experiences: "such phobias
(of horses, dogs, cats, chickens and other domestic animals) are, I think, at least as prevalent as
*pavor nocturnus* in childhood, and usually reveal
themselves in the analysis as a displacement of
fear from one of the parents to animals. I am
not prepared to assert that the wide-spread mouse
and rat phobia has the same mechanism."

I reported the "Analysis of the Phobia of a
five-year-old Boy" [59] which the father of the
little patient had put at my disposal. It was a
fear of horses as a result of which the boy refused
to go on the street. He expressed his apprehen-
sion that the horse would come into the room and
bite him. It proved that this was meant to be

[58a] M. Wulff, "Contributions to Infantile Sexuality," Zentralbl.
f. Psychoanalyze, 1912, II, Nr. I, p. 15.
[59] "Little Hans," translated by A. A. Brill, Moffat, Yard & Co.

the punishment for his wish that the horse should fall over (die). After assurances had relieved the boy of his fear of his father, it proved that he was fighting against wishes whose content was the absence (departure or death) of the father. He indicated only too plainly that he felt the father to be his rival for the favor of the mother, upon whom his budding sexual wishes were by dark premonitions directed. He therefore had the typical attitude of the male child to its parents which we call the "Oedipus complex" in which we recognize the central complex of the neuroses in general. Through the analysis of "Little John" we have learnt a fact which is very valuable in relation to totemism, namely, that under such conditions the child displaces a part of its feelings from the father upon some animal.

Analysis showed the paths of association, both significant and accidental in content, along which such a displacement took place. It also allowed one to guess the motives for the displacement. The hate which resulted from the rivalry for the mother could not permeate the boy's psychic life without being inhibited; he had to contend with the tenderness and admiration which he had felt for his father from the beginning, so that the child assumed a double or ambivalent emotional attitude towards the father and relieved himself of this ambivalent conflict by displacing his hostile and anxious feelings upon a substitute for the father. The displacement could not, however, relieve the conflict by bringing about a smooth division between the tender and the hostile feelings. On the contrary, the conflict was continued in reference to the object to which displacement has been made and to which also the ambivalence spreads. There was no doubt that little John had not only fear, but respect and interest for horses. As soon as his fear was moderated he identified himself with the feared animal; he jumped around like a horse, and now it was he who bit the father.[60] In another stage of solution of the phobia he did not scruple to identify his parents with other large animals.[61]

We may venture the impression that certain traits of totemism return as a negative expression in these animal phobias of children. But we are indebted to S. Ferenczi for a beautiful individual observation of what must be called a case of positive totemism in the child.[62] It is true that with the little Arpád, whom Ferenczi reports, the totemic interests do not awaken in direct connection with the Oedipus complex, but on the basis of a narcistic premise, namely, the

[60] l. c., p. 41.
[61] "The Phantasy of the Giraffe," l. c., p. 30.
[62] S. Ferenczi, "Contributions to Psychoanalysis," p. 204, translated by Ernest Jones, R. G. Badger, Boston, 1916.

fear of castration. But whoever looks atten-
tively through the history of little John will also
find there abundant proof that the father was
admired as the possessor of large genitals and
was feared as threatening the child's own genitals. In the Oedipus as well as in the castration
complex the father plays the same rôle of feared
opponent to the infantile sexual interests. Castration and its substitute through blinding is the
punishment he threatens.[63]

When little Arpád was two and a half years
old he once tried, while at a summer resort,
to urinate into the chicken coop, and on this
occasion a chicken bit his penis or snapped at
it. When he returned to the same place a year
later he became a chicken himself, was interested only in the chicken coop and in everything that occurred there, and gave up human
speech for cackling and crowing. During the
period of observation, at the age of five, he spoke
again, but his speech was exclusively about
chickens and other fowl. He played with no
other toy and sang only songs in which there was
something about poultry. His behavior towards his totem animal was subtly ambivalent,
expressing itself in immoderate hating and

[63] Compare the communications of Reitler, Ferenczi, Rank and
Eder about the substitution of blindness in the Oedipus myth for
castration. Intern. Zeitschrift f. arzte. Psychoanalyze, 1913, I,
No. 2.

loving. He loved best to play killing chickens. "The slaughtering of poultry was quite a festival for him. He could dance around the animals' bodies for hours at a time in a state of intense excitement." [64] But then he kissed and stroked the slaughtered animal, and cleaned and caressed the chicken effigies which he himself had ill-used.

Arpád himself saw to it that the meaning of his curious activity could not remain hidden. At times he translated his wishes from the totemic method of expression back into that of everyday life. "Now I am small, now I am a chicken. When I get bigger I shall be a fowl. When I am bigger still, I shall be a cock." On another occasion he suddenly expressed the wish to eat a "potted mother," (by analogy, potted fowl). He was very free with open threats of castration against others, just as he himself had received them on account of onanistic preoccupation with his penis.

According to Ferenczi there was no doubt as to the source of his interest in the activities of the chicken yard: "The continual sexual activity between cock and hen, the laying of eggs and the creeping out of the young brood" [65] satisfied his sexual curiosity which really was directed towards human family life. His object wishes

[64] Ferenczi, l. c., p. 209.    [65] Ferenczi, l. c., p. 212.

have been formed on the model of chicken life when we find him saying to a woman neighbor: "I am going to marry you and your sister and my three cousins and the cook; no, instead of the cook I'll marry my mother."

We shall be able to complete our consideration of these observations later; at present we will only point out two traits that show a valuable correspondence with totemism: the complete identification with the totem animal,[66] and the ambivalent affective attitude towards it. In view of these observations we consider ourselves justified in substituting the father for the totem animal in the male's formula of totemism. We then notice that in doing so we have taken no new or especially daring step. For primitive men say it themselves and, as far as the totemic system is still in effect to-day, the totem is called ancestor and primal father. We have only taken literally an expression of these races which ethnologists did not know what to do with and were therefore inclined to put it into the background. Psychoanalysis warns us, on the contrary, to emphasize this very point and to connect it with the attempt to explain totemism.[67]

[66] Frazer finds that the essence of totemism is in this identification: "Totemism is an identification of a man with his totem." "Totemism and Exogamy," IV, p. 5.

[67] I am indebted to Otto Rank for the report of a case of dog phobia in an intelligent young man whose explanation of how he

The first result of our substitution is very remarkable. If the totem animal is the father, then the two main commandments of totemism, the two taboo rules which constitute its nucleus,—not to kill the totem animal and not to use a woman belonging to the same totem for sexual purposes,—agree in content with the two crimes of Oedipus, who slew his father and took his mother to wife, and also with the child's two primal wishes whose insufficient repression or whose re-awakening forms the nucleus of perhaps all neuroses. If this similarity is more than a deceptive play of accident it would perforce make it possible for us to shed light upon the origin of totemism in prehistoric times. In other words, we should succeed in making it probable that the totemic system resulted from the conditions underlying the Oedipus complex, just as the animal phobia of "little John" and the poultry perversion of "little Arpád" resulted from it. In order to trace this possibility we shall in what follows study a peculiarity of the totemic system or, as we may say, of the totemic religion, which until now could hardly be brought into the discussion.

acquired his ailment sounds remarkably like the totem theory of the Aruntas mentioned above. He had heard from his father that his mother at one time during her pregnancy had been frightened by a dog.

4

W. Robertson Smith, who died in 1894, was a physicist, philologist, Bible critic, and archæ- ologist, a many-sided as well as keen and free thinking man, expressed the assumption in his work on the "Religion of the Semites," [68] pub- lished in 1889, that a peculiar ceremony, the so- called *totem feast,* had, from the very beginning, formed an integral part of the totemic system. For the support of this supposition he had at his disposal at that time only a single description of such an act from the year 500 A. D.; he knew, however, how to give a high degree of probability to his assumption through his analysis of the nature of sacrifice among the old Semites. As sacrifice assumes a godlike person we are dealing here with an inference from a higher phase of religious rite to its lowest phase in totemism.

I shall now cite from Robertson Smith's ex- cellent book [69] those statements about the origin and meaning of the sacrificial rite which are of great interest to us; I shall omit the only too numerous tempting details as well as the parts dealing with all later developments. In such an excerpt it is quite impossible to give the

[68] "The Religion of the Semites,' Second Edition, London, 1907.
[69] W. Robertson Smith, "The Religion of the Semites," 2d Edi- tion, London, 1907.

reader any sense of the lucidity or of the argumentative force of the original.

Robertson Smith shows that sacrifice at the altar was the essential part of the rite of old religions. It plays the same rôle in all religions, so that its origin must be traced back to very general causes whose effects were everywhere the same.

But the sacrifice—the holy action κατἐζογη (sacrificium ἱερουργία)—originally meant something different from what later times understood by it: the offering to the deity in order to reconcile him or to incline him to be favorable. The profane use of the word was afterwards derived from the secondary sense of self-denial. As is demonstrated the first sacrifice was nothing else than "an act of social fellowship between the deity and his worshipers."

Things to eat and drink were brought as sacrifice; man offered to his god the same things on which he himself lived, flesh, cereals, fruits, wine and oil. Only in regard to the sacrificial flesh did there exist restrictions and exceptions. The god partakes of the animal sacrifices with his worshipers while the vegetable sacrifices are left to him alone. There is no doubt that animal sacrifices are older and at one time were the only forms of sacrifice. The vegetable sacrifices resulted from the offering of the first-fruits and correspond to a tribute to the lord of the soil and the land. But animal sacrifice is older than agriculture.

Linguistic survivals make it certain that the part of the sacrifice destined for the god was looked upon as his real food. This conception became offensive with the progressive dematerialization of the deity, and was avoided by offering the deity only the liquid part of the meal. Later the use of fire, which made the sacrificial flesh ascend in smoke from the altar, made it possible to prepare human food in such a way that it was more suitable for the deity. The drink sacrifice was originally the blood of the sacrificed animals; wine was used later as a substitute for the blood. Primitive man looked upon wine as the "blood of the grape," as our poets still call it.

The oldest form of sacrifice, older than the use of fire and the knowledge of agriculture, was therefore the sacrifice of animals, whose flesh and blood the god and his worshipers ate together. It was essential that both participants should receive their share of the meal.

Such a sacrifice was a public ceremony, the celebration of a whole clan. As a matter of fact all religion was a public affair, religious duty was a part of the social obligation. Sacrifice and festival go together among all races, each sacrifice entails a holiday and no holiday can be celebrated without a sacrifice. The sacrificial festival was an occasion for joyously transcending one's own interests and emphasizing social community and community with god.

The ethical power of the public sacrificial feast was based upon primal conceptions of the meaning of eating and drinking in common. To eat and drink with some one was at the same time a symbol and a confirmation of social community and of the assumption of mutual obligations; the sacrificial eating gave direct expression to the fact that the god and his worshipers are communicants, thus confirming all their other relations. Customs that to-day still are in force among the Arabs of the desert prove that the binding force resulting from the common meal is not a religious factor but that the subsequent mutual obligations are due to the act of eating itself. Whoever has shared the smallest bite with such a Beduin, or has taken a swallow of his milk, need not fear him any longer as an enemy, but may be sure of his protection and help. Not indeed, forever, strictly speaking this lasts only while it may be assumed that the food partaken remains in the body. So realistically is the bond of union conceived; it requires repetition to strengthen it and make it endure.

But why is this binding power ascribed to

eating and drinking in common? In the most primitive societies there is only one unconditional and never failing bond, that of kinship. The members of a community stand by each other jointly and severally, a kin is a group of persons whose life is so bound into a physical unity that they can be considered as parts of a common life. In case of the murder of one of this kin they therefore do not say: the blood of so and so has been spilt, but our blood has been spilt. The Hebraic phrase by which the tribal relation is acknowledged is: "Thou art my bone and my flesh." Kinship therefore signifies having part in a general substance. It is natural then that it is based not only upon the fact that we are a part of the substance of our mother who has borne us, and whose milk nourished us, but also that the food eaten later through which the body is renewed, can acquire and strengthen kinship. If one shared a meal with one's god the conviction was thus expressed that one was of the same substance as he, no meal was therefore partaken with any one recognized as a stranger.

The sacrificial repast was therefore originally a feast of the kin, following the rule that only those of kin could eat together. In our society the meal unites the members of the family; but the sacrificial repast has nothing to do with the family. Kinship is older than family life; the oldest families known to us regularly comprised persons who belonged to various bonds of kinship. The men married women of strange clans and the children inherited the clan of the mother; there was no kinship between the man and the rest of the members of the family. In such a family there was no common meal. Even to-day savages eat apart and alone, and the religious prohibitions of totemism as to eating often make it impossible for them to eat with their wives and children.

Let us now turn to the sacrificial animal. There was, as we have heard, no meeting of the kin without animal sacrifice, but, and this is significant, no animal was slaughtered except for such a solemn occasion. Without any hesitation the people ate fruits, game and the milk of domestic animals, but religious scruples made it impossible for the individual to kill a domestic animal for his own use. There is not the least doubt, says Robertson Smith, that every sacrifice was originally a clan sacrifice, and that the *killing of a sacrificial animal* originally belonged to those acts which were *forbidden to the individual and were only justified if the whole kin assumed the responsibility.* Primitive men had only one class of actions which were thus characterized, namely, actions which touched the holiness of the kin's common blood. A life which no individual might take and which could be sacrificed only through the consent and participation of all the members of the clan was on the same plane as the life of a member of the kin. The rule that every guest of the sacrificial repast must partake of the flesh of the sacrificial animal, had the same meaning as the rule that the execution of a guilty member of the kin must be performed by the whole kin. In other words: the sacrificial animal was treated like one of kin; *the sacrificing community, its god, and the sacrificial animal were of the same blood,* and the members of a clan.

On the basis of much evidence Robertson Smith identifies the sacrificial animal with the old totem animal. In a later age there were two kinds of sacrifices, those of domestic animals which usually were also eaten, and the unusual sacrifice of animals which were forbidden as being unclean. Further investigation then shows that these unclean animals were holy and that they were sacrificed to the gods to whom they were holy, that these animals were originally identified with the gods themselves and that at the sacrifice the worshipers in some way emphasized their blood relationship to the god and to the animal. But this difference between usual and "mystic" sacrifices does not hold good for still earlier times. Originally all animals were holy, their meat was forbidden and might be eaten only on solemn occasions, with the participation of the whole kin. The slaughter of the animal amounted to the spilling of the kin's blood and had to be done with the same precautions and assurances against reproach.

The taming of domestic animals and the rise of cattle-breeding seems everywhere to have put an end to the pure and rigorous totemism of earliest times.[70] But such holiness as still clung to domestic animals in what was now a "pastoral" religion, is sufficiently distinct for us to recognize its totemic character. Even in late classical times the rite in several localities prescribed flight for the sacrificer after the sacrifice, as if to escape revenge. In Greece the idea must once have been general that the killing of an ox was really a crime. At the Athenian festival of the Bouphonia a formal trial to which all the participants were summoned, was instituted after the sacrifice. Finally it was agreed to put the blame for the murder upon the knife, which was then cast into the sea.

In spite of the dread which protects the life of the animal as being of kin, it became necessary

[70] "The inference is that the domestication to which totemism leads (when there are any animals capable of domestication) is fatal to totemism." Jevons, "An Introduction to the History of Religion," 1911, fifth edition, p. 120.

to kill it from time to time in solemn conclave, and to divide its flesh and blood among the members of the clan. The motive which commands this act reveals the deepest meaning of the essence of sacrifice. We have heard that in later times every eating in common, the participation in the same substance which entered into their bodies, established a holy bond between the communicants; in oldest times this meaning seemed to be attached only to participation in the substance of a holy sacrifice. *The holy mystery of the sacrificial death was justified in that only in this way could the holy bond be established which united the participants with each other and with their god.*[71]

This bond was nothing else than the life of the sacrificial animal which lived on its flesh and blood and was shared by all the participants by means of the sacrificial feast. Such an idea was the basis of all the *blood bonds* through which men in still later times became pledged to each other. The thoroughly realistic conception of consanguinity as an identity of substance makes comprehensible the necessity of renewing it from time to time through the physical process of the sacrificial repast.

We will now stop quoting from Robertson Smith's train of thought in order to give a

[71] l. c., p. 313.

condensed summary of what is essential in it.
When the idea of private property came into
existence sacrifice was conceived as a gift to the
deity, as a transfer from the property of man
to that of the god. But this interpretation left
all the peculiarities of the sacrificial ritual unexplained. In oldest times the sacrificial animal
itself had been holy and its life inviolate; it could
be taken only in the presence of the god, with the
whole tribe taking part and sharing the guilt in
order to furnish the holy substance through the
eating of which the members of the clan assured
themselves of their material identity with each
other and with the deity. The sacrifice was a
sacrament, and the sacrificial animal itself was
one of the kin. In reality it was the old totem
animal, the primitive god himself through the
slaying and eating of whom the members of the
clan revived and assured their similarity with the
god.

From this analysis of the nature of sacrifice
Robertson Smith drew the conclusion that the
periodic killing and eating of the totem before
the period when *the anthropomorphic deities
were venerated* was an important part of totem
religion. The ceremonial of such a totem feast
was preserved for us, he thought, in the description of a sacrifice in later times. Saint
Nilus tells of a sacrificial custom of the Beduins

in the desert of Sinai towards the end of the
fourth century A. D. The victim, a camel, was
bound and laid upon a rough altar of stones; the
leader of the tribe made the participants walk
three times around the altar to the accompani-
ment of song, inflicted the first wound upon the
animal and greedily drank the spurting blood;
then the whole community threw itself upon the
sacrifice, cut off pieces of the palpitating flesh
with their swords and ate them raw in such haste
that in a short interval between the rise of the
morning star, for whom this sacrifice was meant,
and its fading before the rays of the sun, the
whole sacrificial, animal, flesh, skin, bones, and
entrails, were devoured. According to every
testimony this barbarous rite, which speaks of
great antiquity, was not a rare custom but the
general original form of the totem sacrifice,
which in later times underwent the most varied
modifications.

Many authors have refused to grant any
weight to this conception of the totem feast because it could not be strengthened by direct observation at the stage of totemism. Robertson
Smith himself has referred to examples in which
the sacramental meaning of sacrifices seems certain, such as the human sacrifices of the Aztecs
and others which recall the conditions of the
totem feast, the bear sacrifices of the bear tribe

of the *Ouataouaks* in America, and the bear festival of the Ainus in Japan. Frazer has given
a full account of these and similar cases in the
two divisions of his great work that have last
appeared.[72] An Indian tribe in California
which reveres the buzzard, a large bird of prey,
kills it once a year with solemn ceremony, where-
upon the bird is mourned and its skin and feath-
ers preserved. The Zuni Indians in New
Mexico do the same thing with their holy turtle.

In the *Intichiuma* ceremonies of Central Australian tribes a trait has been observed which fits
in excellently with the assumptions of Robertson
Smith. Every tribe that practices magic for
the increase of its totem, which it cannot eat
itself, is bound to eat a part of its totem at the
ceremony before it can be touched by the other
tribes. According to Frazer the best example
of the sacramental consumption of the otherwise
forbidden totem is to be found among the Bini
in West Africa, in connection with the burial
ceremony of this tribe.[73]

But we shall follow Robertson Smith in the
assumption that the sacramental killing and the
common consumption of the otherwise forbidden

[72] "The Golden Bough," Part V, "Spirits of the Corn and of the
Wild," 1912, in the chapters: "Eating the God and Killing the
Divine Animal."

[73] Frazer, "Totem and Exogamy," Vol. II, p. 590.

totem animal was an important trait of the totem
religion.[74]

## 5

Let us now envisage the scene of such a totem
meal and let us embellish it further with a few
probable features which could not be adequately
considered before. Thus we have the clan,
which on a solemn occasion kills its totem in a
cruel manner and eats it raw, blood, flesh, and
bones. At the same time the members of the
clan, disguised in imitation of the totem, mimic
it in sound and movement as if they wanted to
emphasize their common identity. There is also
the conscious realization that an action is being
carried out which is forbidden to each individual
and which can only be justified through the participation of all, so that no one is allowed to exclude himself from the killing and the feast.
After the act is accomplished the murdered animal is bewailed and lamented. The death lamentation is compulsive, being enforced by the
fear of a threatening retribution, and its main
purpose is, as Robertson Smith remarks on an
analogous occasion, to exculpate oneself from
responsibility for the slaying.[75]

[74] I am not ignorant of the objections to this theory of sacrifice
as expressed by Marillier, Hubert, Mauss and others, but they
have not essentially impaired the theories of Robertson Smith.

[75] "Religion of the Semites," 2nd Edition, 1907, p. 412.

But after this mourning there follows loud festival gaiety accompanied by the unchaining of every impulse and the permission of every gratification. Here we find an easy insight into the nature of the *holiday*.

A holiday is a permitted, or rather a prescribed excess, a solemn violation of a prohibition. People do not commit the excesses which at all times have characterized holidays, as a result of an order to be in a holiday mood, but because in the very nature of a holiday there is excess; the holiday mood is brought about by the release of what is otherwise forbidden.

But what has mourning over the death of the totem animal to do with the introduction of this holiday spirit? If men are happy over the slaying of the totem, which is otherwise forbidden to them, why do they also mourn it?

We have heard that members of a clan become holy through the consumption of the totem and thereby also strengthen their identification with it and with each other. The fact that they have absorbed the holy life with which the substance of the totem is charged may explain the holiday mood and everything that results from it.

Psychoanalysis has revealed to us that the totem animal is really a substitute for the father, and this really explains the contradiction that it is usually forbidden to kill the totem animal, that the killing of it results in a holiday and that the animal is killed and yet mourned. The ambivalent emotional attitude which to-day still marks the father complex in our children and so often continues into adult life also extended to the father substitute of the totem animal.

But if we associate the translation of the totem as given by psychoanalysis, with the totem feast and the Darwinian hypothesis about the primal state of human society, a deeper understanding becomes possible and a hypothesis is offered which may seem phantastic but which has the advantage of establishing an unexpected unity among a series of hitherto separated phenomena.

The Darwinian conception of the primal horde does not, of course, allow for the beginnings of totemism. There is only a violent, jealous father who keeps all the females for himself and drives away the growing sons. This primal state of society has nowhere been observed. The most primitive organization we know, which to-day is still in force with certain tribes, is *associations of men* consisting of members with equal rights, subject to the restrictions of the totemic system, and founded on matriarchy, or descent through the mother.[76] Can the one have re-

---

[76] For a recent contribution compare, "The Whole House of The Chilkat," by G. T. Emmons, *American Museum Journal*, Vol. XVI, No. 7. (Translator.)

sulted from the other, and how was this possible?

By basing our argument upon the celebration of the totem we are in a position to give an answer: One day [77] the expelled brothers joined forces, slew and ate the father, and thus put an end to the father horde. Together they dared and accomplished what would have remained impossible for them singly. Perhaps some advance in culture, like the use of a new weapon, had given them the feeling of superiority. Of course these cannibalistic savages ate their victim. This violent primal father had surely been the envied and feared model for each of the brothers. Now they accomplished their identification with him by devouring him and each acquired a part of his strength. The totem feast, which is perhaps mankind's first celebration, would be the repetition and commemoration of this memorable, criminal act with which so many things began, social organization, moral restrictions and religion.[78]

[77] The reader will avoid the erroneous impression which this exposition may call forth by taking into consideration the concluding sentence of the subsequent chapter.

[78] The seemingly monstrous assumption that the tyrannical father was overcome and slain by a combination of the expelled sons has also been accepted by Atkinson as a direct result of the conditions of the Darwinian primal horde. "A youthful band of brothers living together in forced celibacy, or at most in polyandrous relation with some single female captive. A horde as yet weak in their impubescence they are, but they would, when strength was gained with time, inevitably wrench by combined

In order to find these results acceptable, quite aside from our supposition, we need only assume that the group of brothers banded together were dominated by the same contradictory feelings towards the father which we can demonstrate as the content of ambivalence of the father complex in all our children and in neurotics. They hated the father who stood so powerfully in the way of their sexual demands and their desire for power, but they also loved and admired him.

attacks renewed again and again, both wife and life from the paternal tyrant" ("Primal Law," pp. 220-221). Atkinson, who spent his life in New Caledonia and had unusual opportunities to study the natives, also refers to the fact that the conditions of the primal horde which Darwin assumes can easily be observed among herds of wild cattle and horses and regularly lead to the killing of the father animal. He then assumes further that a disintegration of the horde took place after the removal of the father through embittered fighting among the victorious sons, which thus precluded the origin of a new organization of society: "An ever recurring violent succession to the solitary paternal tyrant by sons, whose parricidal hands were so soon again clenched in fratricidal strife" (p. 228). Atkinson, who did not have the suggestions of psychoanalysis at his command and did not know the studies of Robertson Smith, finds a less violent transition from the primal horde to the next social stage in which many men live together in peaceful accord. He attributes it to maternal love that at first only the youngest sons and later others too remain in the horde, who in return for this toleration acknowledge the sexual prerogative of the father by the restraint which they practice towards the mother and towards their sisters.

So much for the very remarkable theory of Atkinson, its essential correspondence with the theory here expounded, and its point of departure which makes it necessary to relinquish so much else.

I must ascribe the indefiniteness, the disregard of time interval, and the crowding of the material in the above exposition to a restraint which the nature of the subject demands. It would be just as meaningless to strive for exactness in this material as it would be unfair to demand certainty here.

After they had satisfied their hate by his removal and had carried out their wish for identification with him, the suppressed tender impulses had to assert themselves.[79] This took place in the form of remorse, a sense of guilt was formed which coincided here with the remorse generally felt. The dead now became stronger than the living had been, even as we observe it to-day in the destinies of men. What the father's presence had formerly prevented they themselves now prohibited in the psychic situation of "subsequent obedience" which we know so well from psycho-analysis. They undid their deed by declaring that the killing of the father substitute, the totem, was not allowed, and renounced the fruits of their deed by denying themselves the liberated women. Thus they created the two funda-mental taboos of totemism out of the *sense of guilt of the son,* and for this very reason these had to correspond with the two repressed wishes of the Oedipus complex. Whoever disobeyed became guilty of the two only crimes which troubled primitive society.[80]

[79] This new emotional attitude must also have been responsible for the fact that the deed could not bring full satisfaction to any of the perpetrators. In a certain sense it had been in vain. For none of the sons could carry out his original wish of taking the place of the father. But failure is, as we know, much more favor-able to moral reaction than success.

[80] "Murder and incest, or offences of like kind against the sacred law of blood are in primitive society the only crimes of

The two taboos of totemism with which the
morality of man begins are psychologically not
of equal value.  One of them, the sparing of the
totem animal, rests entirely upon emotional motives; the father had been removed and nothing
in reality could make up for this.  But the other,
the incest prohibition, had, besides, a strong prae-
tical foundation.  Sexual need does not unite
men, it separates them.  Though the brothers
had joined forces in order to overcome the father,
each was the other's rival among the women.
Each one wanted to have them all to himself like
the father, and in the fight of each against the
other the new organization would have perished.
For there was no longer any one stronger than
all the rest who could have successfully assumed
the rôle of the father.  Thus there was nothing
left for the brothers, if they wanted to live
together, but to erect the incest prohibition—perhaps after many difficult experiences—through
which they all equally renounced the women
whom they desired, and on account of whom they
had removed the father in the first place.  Thus
they saved the organization which had made them
strong and which could be based upon the homo-
sexual feelings and activities which probably
manifested themselves among them during the

which the community as such takes cognizance . . ." "Religion of
the Semites," p. 419.

time of their banishment. Perhaps this situation also formed the germ of the institution of the mother right discovered by Bachofen, which was then abrogated by the patriarchal family arrangement.

On the other hand the claim of totemism to be considered the first attempt at a religion is connected with the other taboo which protects the life of the totem animal. The feelings of the sons found a natural and appropriate substitute for the father in the animal, but their compulsory treatment of it expressed more than the need of showing remorse. The surrogate for the father was perhaps used in the attempt to assuage the burning sense of guilt, and to bring about a kind of reconciliation with the father. The totemic system was a kind of agreement with the father in which the latter granted everything that the child's phantasy could expect from him, protection, care, and forbearance, in return for which the pledge was given to honor his life, that is to say, not to repeat the act against the totem through which the real father had perished. Totemism also contained an attempt at justification. "If the father had treated us like the totem we should never have been tempted to kill him." Thus totemism helped to gloss over the real state of affairs and to make one forget the event to which it owed its origin.

In this connection some features were formed which henceforth determined the character of every religion. The totem religion had issued from the sense of guilt of the sons as an attempt to palliate this feeling and to conciliate the injured father through subsequent obedience. All later religions prove to be attempts to solve the same problem, varying only in accordance with the stage of culture in which they are attempted and according to the paths which they take; they are all, however, reactions aiming at the same great event with which culture began and which ever since has not let mankind come to rest.

There is still another characteristic faithfully preserved in religion which already appeared in totemism at this time. The ambivalent strain was probably too great to be adjusted by any arrangement, or else the psychological conditions are entirely unfavorable to any kind of settlement of these contradictory feelings. It is certainly noticeable that the ambivalence attached to the father complex also continues in totemism and in religions in general. The religion of totemism included not only· manifestations of remorse and attempts at reconciliation, but also serves to commemorate the triumph over the father. The gratification obtained thereby creates the commemorative celebration of the totem feast at which the restrictions of subsequent obedience are suspended, and makes it a duty to repeat the crime of parricide through the sacrifice of the totem animal as often as the benefits of this deed, namely, the appropriation of the father's properties, threaten to disappear as a result of the changed influences of life. We shall not be surprised to find that a part of the son's defiance also reappears, often in the most remarkable disguises and inversions, in the formation of later religions.

If thus far we have followed, in religion and moral precepts—but little differentiated in totemism—the consequences of the tender impulses towards the father as they are changed into remorse, we must not overlook the fact that for the most part the tendencies which have impelled to parricide have retained the victory. The social and fraternal feelings on which this great change is based, henceforth for long periods exercises the greatest influence upon the development of society. They find expression in the sanctification of the common blood and in the emphasis upon the solidarity of life within the clan. In thus ensuring each other's lives the brothers express the fact that no one of them is to be treated by the other as they all treated the father. They preclude a repetition of the fate of the father. The socially established prohibition against fratricide is now added to the prohibition against killing the totem, which is based on religious grounds. It will still be a long time before the commandment discards the restriction to members of the tribe and assumes the simple phraseology: Thou shalt not kill. At first the *brother clan* has taken the place of the *father horde* and was guaranteed by the blood bond. Society is now based on complicity in the common crime, religion on the sense of guilt and the consequent remorse, while morality is based partly on the necessities of society and partly on the expiation which this sense of guilt demands.

Thus psychoanalysis, contrary to the newer conceptions of the totemic system and more in accord with older conceptions, bids us argue for an intimate connection between totemism and exogamy ás well as for their simultaneous origin.

## 6

I am under the influence of many strong motives which restrain me from the attempt to discuss the further development of religions from their beginning in totemism up to their present state. I shall follow out only two threads as I see them appearing in the weft with especial distinctness: the motive of the totem sacrifice and the relation of the son to the father.[81]

81 Compare "Transformations and Symbols of the Libido," by C. G. Jung, in which some dissenting points of view are represented.

Robertson Smith has shown us that the old
totem feast returns in the original form of sacrifice. The meaning of the rite is the same:
sanctification through participation in the common meal. The sense of guilt, which can only
be allayed through the solidarity of all the participants, has also been retained. In addition
to this there is the tribal deity in whose supposed
presence the sacrifice takes place, who takes part
in the meal like a member of the tribe, and with
whom identification is effected by the act of eating the sacrifice. How does the god come into
this situation which originally was foreign to
him?

The answer might be that the idea of god had
meanwhile appeared,—no one knows whence—
and had dominated the whole religious life, and
that the totem feast, like everything else that
wished to survive, had been forced to fit itself
into the new system. However, psychoanalytic
investigation of the individual teaches with especial emphasis that god is in every case modeled
after the father and that our personal relation
to god is dependent upon our relation to our
physical father, fluctuating and changing with
him, and that god at bottom is nothing but an
exalted father. Here also, as in the case of
totemism, psychoanalysis advises us to believe
the faithful, who call god father just as they

called the totem their ancestor. If psychoanalysis deserves any consideration at all, then the share of the father in the idea of a god must be very important, quite aside from all the other origins and meanings of god upon which psychoanalysis can throw no light. But then the father would be represented twice in primitive sacrifice, first as god, and secondly as the totem-animal-sacrifice, and we must ask, with all due regard for the limited number of solutions which psychoanalysis offers, whether this is possible and what the meaning of it may be.

We know that there are a number of relations of the god to the holy animal (the totem and the sacrificial animal): 1. Usually one animal is sacred to every god, sometimes even several animals. 2. In certain, especially holy, sacrifices, the so-called "mystical" sacrifices, the very animal which had been sanctified through the god was sacrificed to him.[82] 3. The god was often revered in the form of an animal, or from another point of view, animals enjoyed a godlike reverence long after the period of totemism. 4. In myths the god is frequently transformed into an animal, often into the animal that is sacred to him. From this the assumption was obvious that the god himself was the animal, and that he had evolved from the totem animal at a later

[82] Robertson Smith, "Religion of the Semites."

stage of religious feeling. But the reflection
that the totem itself is nothing but a substitute
for the father relieves us of all further discussion.
Thus the totem may have been the first form of
the father substitute and the god a later one in
which the father regained his human form. Such
a new creation from the root of all religious evolution, namely, the longing for the father, might
become possible if in the course of time an essential change had taken place in the relation to the
father and perhaps also to the animal.

Such changes are easily divined even if we disregard the beginning of a psychic estrangement
from the animal as well as the disintegration of
totemism through animal domestication.[83] The
situation created by the removal of the father
contained an element which in the course of time
must have brought about an extraordinary increase of longing for the father. For the brothers who had joined forces to kill the father had
each been animated by the wish to become like
the father and had given expression to this wish
by incorporating parts of the substitute for him
in the totem feast. In consequence of the pressure which the bonds of the brother clan exercised upon each member, this wish had to remain
unfulfilled. No one could or was allowed to attain the father's perfection of power, which was

[83] See above, p. 127.

the thing they had all sought. Thus the bitter feeling against the father which had incited to the deed could subside in the course of time, while the longing for him grew, and an ideal could arise having as a content the fullness of power and the freedom from restriction of the conquered primal father, as well as the willingness to subject themselves to him. The original democratic equality of each member of the tribe could no longer be retained on account of the interference of cultural changes; in consequence of which there arose a tendency to revive the old father ideal in the creation of gods through the veneration of those individuals who had distinguished themselves above the rest. That a man should become a god and that a god should die, which to-day seems to us an outrageous presumption, was still by no means offensive to the conceptions of classical antiquity.[84] But the deification of the murdered father from whom the tribe now derived its origin, was a much more serious attempt at expiation than the former covenant with the totem.

[84] "To us moderns, for whom the breach which divides the human and divine has deepened into an impassable gulf, such mimicry may appear impious, but it was otherwise with the ancients. To their thinking gods and men were akin, for many families traced their descent from a divinity, and the deification of a man probably seemed as little extraordinary to them as the canonization of a saint seems to a modern Catholic." Frazer, "The Golden Bough," I; "The Magic Art and the Evolution of Kings," II, p. 177.

In this evolution I am at a loss to indicate the place of the great maternal deities who perhaps everywhere preceded the paternal deities. But it seems certain that the change in the relation to the father was not restricted to religion but logically extended to the other side of human life influenced by the removal of the father, namely, the social organization. With the institution of paternal deities the fatherless society gradually changed into a patriarchal one. The family was a reconstruction of the former primal horde and also restored a great part of their former rights to the fathers. Now there were patriarchs again but the social achievements of the brother clan had not been given up and the actual difference between the new family patriarchs and the unrestricted primal father was great enough to insure the continuation of the religious need, the preservation of the unsatisfied longing for the father.

The father therefore really appears twice in the scene of sacrifice before the tribal god, once as the god and again as the totem-sacrificial-animal. But in attempting to understand this situation we must beware of interpretations which superficially seek to translate it as an allegory, and which forget the historical stages in the process. The twofold presence of the father corresponds to the two successive meanings of the scene. The ambivalent attitude towards the father as well as the victory of the son's tender emotional feelings over his hostile ones, have here found plastic expression. The scene of vanquishing the father, his greatest degradation, furnishes here the material to represent his highest triumph. The meaning which sacrifice has quite generally acquired is found in the fact that in the very same action which continues the memory of this misdeed it offers satisfaction to the father for the ignominy put upon him.

In the further development the animal loses its sacredness and the sacrifice its relation to the celebration of the totem; the rite becomes a simple offering to the deity, a self-deprivation in favor of the god. God himself is now so exalted above man that he can be communicated with only through a priest as intermediary. At the same time the social order produces godlike kings who transfer the patriarchal system to the state. It must be said that the revenge of the deposed and reinstated father has been very cruel; it culminated in the dominance of authority. The subjugated sons have used the new relation to disburden themselves still more of their sense of guilt. Sacrifice, as it is now constituted, is entirely beyond their responsibility. God himself has demanded and ordained it. Myths in which the god himself kills the animal that is

sacred to him, which he himself really is, belong
to this phase. This is the greatest possible denial of the great misdeed with which society and
the sense of guilt began. There is an unmistakable second meaning in this sacrificial demon-
stration. It expresses satisfaction at the fact
that the earlier father substitute has been abandoned in favor of the higher conception of god.
The superficial allegorical translation of the
scene here roughly corresponds with its psychoanalytic interpretation by saying that the god
is represented as overcoming the animal part of
his nature.[85]

But it would be erroneous to believe that in
this period of renewed patriarchal authority the
hostile impulses which belong to the father complex had entirely subsided. On the contrary,
the first phases in the domination of the two new
substitutive formations for the father, those of
gods and kings, plainly show the most ener-
getic expression of that ambivalence which is
characteristic of religion.

[85] It is known that the overcoming of one generation of gods by
another in mythology represents the historical process of the substitution of one religious system by another, either as the result
of conquest by a strange race or by means of a psychological
development. In the latter case the myth approaches the
"functional phenomena" in H. Silberer's sense. That the god
who kills the animal is a symbol of the libido, as asserted by
C. G. Jung (l. c.), presupposes a different conception of the
libido from that hitherto held, and at any rate seems to me
questionable.

In his great work, "The Golden Bough,"
Frazer has expressed the conjecture that the first
kings of the Latin tribes were strangers who
played the part of a deity and were solemnly
sacrificed in this rôle on specified holidays. The
yearly sacrifice (self-sacrifice is a variant) of a
god seems to have been an important feature of
Semitic religions. The ceremony of human sacrifice in various parts of the inhabited world
makes it certain that these human beings ended
their lives as representatives of the deity. This
sacrificial custom can still be traced in later times
in the substitution of an inanimate imitation
(doll) for the living person. The theanthropic
god sacrifice into which unfortunately I cannot
enter with the same thoroughness with which the
animal sacrifice has been treated throws the clear-
est light upon the meaning of the older forms of
sacrifice. It acknowledges with unsurpassable
candor that the object of the sacrificial action has
always been the same, being identical with what
is now revered as a god, namely with the father.
The question as to the relation of animal to
human sacrifice can now be easily solved. The
original animal sacrifice was already a substitute
for a human sacrifice, for the solemn killing of the
father, and when the father substitute regained
its human form, the animal substitute could
also be retransformed into a human sacrifice.

Thus the memory of that first great act of sacrifice had proved to be indestructible despite all attempts to forget it, and just at the moment when men strove to get as far away as possible from its motives, the undistorted repetition of it had to appear in the form of the god sacrifice. I need not fully indicate here the developments of religious thought which made this return possible in the form of rationalizations. Robertson Smith who is, of course, far removed from the idea of tracing sacrifice back to this great event of man's primal history, says that the ceremony of the festivals in which the old Semites celebrated the death of a deity were interpreted as a "commemoration of a mythical tragedy" and that the attendant lament was not characterized by spontaneous sympathy, but displayed a compulsive character, something that was imposed by the fear of a divine wrath.[86] We are in a position to acknowledge that this interpretation was correct, the feelings of the celebrants being well explained by the basic situation.

We may now accept it as a fact that in the

[86] "Religion of the Semites," pp. 412–413. "The mourning is not a spontaneous expression of sympathy with the divine tragedy, but obligatory and enforced by fear of supernatural anger. And a chief object of the mourners is *to disclaim responsibility for the god's death*—a point which has already come before us in connection with theanthropic sacrifices, such as the 'ox-murder at Athens.'"

further development of religions these two inciting factors, the son's sense of guilt and his defiance, were never again extinguished. Every attempted solution of the religious problem and every kind of reconciliation of the two opposing psychic forces gradually falls to the ground, probably under the combined influence of cultural changes, historical events, and inner psychic transformations.

The endeavor of the son to put himself in place of the father god, appeared with greater and greater distinctness. With the introduction of agriculture the importance of the son in the patriarchal family increased. He was emboldened to give new expression to his incestuous libido which found symbolic satisfaction in laboring over mother earth. There came into existence figures of gods like Attis, Adonis, Tammuz, and others, spirits of vegetation as well as youthful divinities who enjoyed the favors of maternal deities and committed incest with the mother in defiance of the father. But the sense of guilt which was not allayed through these creations, was expressed in myths which visited these youthful lovers of the maternal goddesses with short life and punishment through castration or through the wrath of the father god appearing in animal form. Adonis was killed by the boar, the sacred animal of Aphrodite; Attis, the lover of Kybele, died of castration.[87]  The lamentation for these gods and the joy at their resurrection have gone over into the ritual of another son which divinity was destined to survive long.

When Christianity began its entry into the ancient world it met with the competition of the religion of Mithras and for a long time it was doubtful which deity was to be the victor.

The bright figure of the youthful Persian god has eluded our understanding.  Perhaps we may conclude from the illustrations of Mithras slaying the steers that he represented the son who carried out the sacrifice of the father by himself and thus released the brothers from their oppressing complicity in the deed.  There was another way of allaying this sense of guilt and this is the one that Christ took.  He sacrificed

[87] The fear of castration plays an extraordinarily big rôle in disturbing the relations to the father in the case of our youthful neurotics.  In Ferenczi's excellent study we have seen how the boy recognized his totem in the animal which snaps at his little penis.  When children learn about ritual circumcision they identify it with castration.  To my knowledge the parallel in the psychology of races to this attitude of our children has not yet been drawn.  The circumcision which was so frequent in primordial times among primitive races belongs to the period of initiation in which its meaning is to be found; it has only secondarily been relegated to an earlier time of life.  It is very interesting that among primitive men circumcision is combined with or replaced by the cutting off of the hair and the drawing of teeth, and that our children, who cannot know anything about this, really treat these two operations as equivalents to castration when they display their fear of them.

his own life and thereby redeemed the brothers from primal sin.

The theory of primal sin is of Orphic origin; it was preserved in the mysteries and thence penetrated into the philosophic schools of Greek antiquity.[88] Men were the descendants of Titans, who had killed and dismembered the young Dionysos-Zagreus; the weight of this crime oppressed them. A fragment of Anaximander says that the unity of the world was destroyed by a primordial crime and everything that issued from it must carry on the punishment for this crime.[89] Although the features of banding together, killing, and dismembering as expressed in the deed of the Titans very clearly recall the totem sacrifice described by St. Nilus— as also many other myths of antiquity, for example, the death of Orpheus himself—we are nevertheless disturbed here by the variation according to which a youthful god was murdered.

In the Christian myth man's original sin is undoubtedly an offense against God the Father, and if Christ redeems mankind from the weight of original sin by sacrificing his own life, he forces us to the conclusion that this sin was murder. According to the law of retaliation which is deeply rooted in human feeling, a mur-

---

[88] Reinach, "Cultes, Mythes, et Religions," II, p. 75.
[89] "Une sorte de péché proethnique," l. c., p. 76.

der can be atoned only by the sacrifice of another life; the self-sacrifice points to a blood-guilt.[90] And if this sacrifice of one's own life brings about a reconciliation with god, the father, then the crime which must be expiated can only have been the murder of the father.

Thus in the Christian doctrine mankind most unreservedly acknowledges the guilty deed of primordial times because it now has found the most complete expiation for this deed in the sacrificial death of the son. The reconciliation with the father is the more thorough because simultaneously with this sacrifice there follows the complete renunciation of woman, for whose sake mankind rebelled against the father. But now also the psychological fatality of ambivalence demands its rights. In the same deed which offers the greatest possible expiation to the father, the son also attains the goal of his wishes against the father. He becomes a god himself beside or rather in place of his father. The religion of the son succeeds the religion of the father. As a sign of this substitution the old totem feast is revived again in the form of communion in which the band of brothers now eats the flesh and blood of the son and no longer that of the father, the sons thereby identifying them-

[90] The suicidal impulses of our neurotics regularly prove to be self-punishments for death wishes directed against others.

selves with him and becoming holy themselves. Thus through the ages we see the identity of the totem feast with the animal sacrifice, the thean-thropic human sacrifice, and the Christian euch-arist, and in all these solemn occasions we recog-nize the after-effects of that crime which so op-pressed men but of which they must have been so proud. At bottom, however, the Christian com-munion is a new setting aside of the father, a rep-etition of the crime that must be expiated. We see how well justified is Frazer's dictum that "the Christian communion has absorbed within itself a sacrament which is doubtless far older than Christianity." [91]

## 7

A process like the removal of the primal father by the band of brothers must have left ineradi-cable traces in the history of mankind and must have expressed itself the more frequently in numerous substitutive formations the less it itself was to be remembered.[92] I am avoiding the

[91] "Eating the God," p. 51. . . . Nobody familiar with the litera-ture on this subject will assume that the tracing back of the Christian communion to the totem feast is an idea of the author of this book.

[92] Ariel in "The Tempest":
> Full fathom five thy father lies:
> Of his bones are coral made;
> Those are pearls that were his eyes;
> Nothing of him that doth fade
> But doth suffer a sea-change
> Into something rich and strange. . . .

temptation of pointing out these traces in mythology, where they are not hard to find, and am
turning to another field in following a hint of S.
Reinach in his suggestive treatment of the death
of Orpheus.[93]

There is a situation in the history of Greek art
which is strikingly familiar even if profoundly
divergent, to the scene of a totem feast discovered by Robertson Smith. It is the situation of
the oldest Greek tragedy. A group of persons,
all of the same name and dressed in the same
way, surround a single figure upon whose words
and actions they are dependent, to represent the
chorus, and the original single impersonator of
the hero. Later developments created a second
and a third actor in order to represent opponents
in playing, and off-shoots of the hero, but the
character of the hero as well as his relation to
the chorus remains unchanged. The hero of the
tragedy had to suffer, this is to-day still the essential content of a tragedy. He had taken upon
himself the so-called "tragic guilt," which is not
always easy to explain; it is often not a guilt in
the ordinary sense. Almost always it consisted
of a rebellion against a divine or human authority
and the chorus accompanied the hero with their
sympathies, trying to restrain and warn him, and

[93] La Mort d'Orphée, "Cultes, Mythes, et Religions," Vol. II, p.
100.

lamented his fate after he had met with what was considered fitting punishment for his daring attempt.

-But why did the hero of the tragedy have to suffer, and what was the meaning of his "tragic" guilt?  We will cut short the discussion by a prompt answer.  He had to suffer because he was the primal father, the hero of that primordial tragedy the repetition of which here serves a certain tendency, and the tragic guilt is the guilt which he had to take upon himself in order to free the chorus of theirs.  The scene upon the stage came into being through purposive distortion of the historical scene or, one is tempted to say, it was the result of refined hypocrisy.  Actually, in the old situation, it was the members of the chorus themselves who had caused the suffering of the hero; here, on the other hand, they exhaust themselves in sympathy and regret, and the hero himself is to blame for his suffering. The crime foisted upon him, namely presumption and rebellion against a great authority, is the same as that which in the past oppressed the colleagues of the chorus, namely, the band of brothers.  Thus the tragic hero, though still against his will, is made the redeemer of the chorus.

When one bears in mind the suffering of the divine goat Dionysos in the performance of the

Greek tragedy and the lament of the retinue of goats who identified themselves with him, one can easily understand how the almost extinct drama was reviewed in the Middle Ages in the Passion of Christ.

In closing this study, which has been carried out in extremely condensed form, I want to state the conclusion that the beginnings of religion, ethics, society, and art meet in the Oedipus complex. This is in entire accord with the findings of psychoanalysis, namely, that the nucleus of all neuroses as far as our present knowledge of them goes is the Oedipus complex. It comes as a great surprise to me that these problems of racial psychology can also be solved through a single concrete instance, such as the relation to the father. Perhaps another psychological problem must be included here. We have so frequently had occasion to show the ambivalence of emotions in its real sense, that is to say the coincidence of love and hate towards the same object, at the root of important cultural formations. We know nothing about the origin of this ambivalence. It may be assumed to be a fundamental phenomenon of our emotional life. But the other possibility seems to me also worthy of consideration: that ambivalence, originally foreign to our emotional life, was acquired by mankind from the father complex,[94] where psychoanalytic investigation of the individual to-day still reveals the strongest expression of it.[95]

Before closing we must take into account that the remarkable convergence reached in these illustrations, pointing to a single inclusive relation, ought not to blind us to the uncertainties of our assumptions and to the difficulties of our conclusions. Of these difficulties I will point out only two which must have forced themselves upon many readers.

In the first place it can hardly have escaped any one that we base everything upon the assumption of a psyche of the mass in which psychic processes occur as in the psychic life of the individual. Moreover, we let the sense of guilt for a deed survive for thousands of years, remaining effective in generations which could not have known anything of this deed. We

[94] That is to say, the parent complex.

[95] I am used to being misunderstood and therefore do not think it superfluous to state clearly that in giving these deductions I am by no means oblivious of the complex nature of the phenomena which give rise to them; the only claim made is that a new factor has been added to the already known or still unrecognized origins of religion, morality, and society, which was furnished through psychoanalytic experience. The synthesis of the whole explanation must be left to another. But it is in the nature of this new contribution that it could play none other than the central rôle in such a synthesis, although it will be necessary to overcome great affective resistances before such importance will be conceded to it.

allow an emotional process such as might have
arisen among generations of sons that had been
ill-treated by their fathers, to continue to new
generations which had escaped such treatment by
the very removal of the father. These seem indeed to be weighty objections and any other explanation which can avoid such assumptions
would seem to merit preference.

But further consideration shows that we ourselves do not have to carry the whole responsibility for such daring. Without the assumption
of a mass psyche, or a continuity in the emotional life of mankind which permits us to disregard the interruptions of psychic acts through
the transgression of individuals, social psychology could not exist at all. If psychic processes
of one generation did not continue in the next,
if each had to acquire its attitude towards life
afresh, there would be no progress in this field
and almost no development. We are now confronted by two new questions: how much can be
attributed to this psychic continuity within the
series of g. nerations, and what ways and means
does a ge. eration use to transfer its psychic
states to the next generation? I do not claim
that these problems have been sufficiently explained or that direct communication and tradition, of which one immediately thinks, are adequate for the task. Social psychology is in gen-

eral little concerned with the manner in which
the required continuity in the psychic life of
succeeding generations is established. A part
of the task seems to be performed by the inheritance of psychic dispositions which, however,
need certain incentives in the individual life in
order to become effective. This may be the
meaning of the poet's words: Strive to possess
yourself of what you have inherited from your
ancestors. The problem would appear more
difficult if we could admit that there are psychic
impulses which can be so completely suppressed
that they leave no traces whatsoever behind them.
But that does not exist. The greatest suppression must leave room for distorted substitutions
and their resulting reactions. But in that case
we may assume that no generation is capable of
concealing its more important psychic processes
from the next. For psychoanalysis has taught
us that in his unconscious psychic activity every
person possesses an apparatus which enables him
to interpret the reactions of others, that is to say,
to straighten out the distortions which the other
person has effected in the expression of his feelings. By this method of unconscious understanding of all customs, ceremonies, and laws
which the original relation to the primal father
had left behind, later generations may also have
succeeded in taking over this legacy of feelings.

There is another objection which the analytic
method of thought itself might raise.

We have interpreted the first rules of morality
and moral restrictions of primitive society as reactions to a deed which gave the authors of it the
conception of crime. They regretted this deed
and decided that it should not be repeated and
that its execution must bring no gain. This cre-
ative sense of guilt has not become extinct with
us. We find its asocial effects in neurotics pro-
ducing new rules of morality and continued
restrictions, in expiation for misdeeds committed,
or as precautions against misdeeds to be committed.[96]   But when we examine these neurotics
for the deeds which have called forth such reactions, we are disappointed. We do not find
deeds, but only impulses and feelings which
sought evil but which were restrained from carrying it out. Only psychic realities and not
actual ones are at the basis of the neurotics' sense
of guilt. It is characteristic of the neurosis to
put a psychic reality above an actual one and to
react as seriously to thoughts as the normal person reacts only towards realities.

May it not be true that the case was somewhat
the same with primitive men? We are justified
in ascribing to them an extraordinary over-valuation of their psychic acts as a partial manifesta-

[96] Compare Chapter II.

tion of their narcistic organization.[97]   According
to this the mere impulses of hostility towards the
father and the existence of the wish phantasy to
kill and devour him may have sufficed to bring
about the moral reaction which has created totemism and taboo.  We should thus escape the necessity of tracing back the beginning of our cultural possession, of which we rightly are so proud,
to a horrible crime which wounds all our feelings.
The causal connection, which stretches from that
beginning to the present time, would not be impaired, for the psychic reality would be of sufficient importance to account for all these consequences.  It may be agreed that a change has
really taken place in the form of society from
the father horde to the brother clan.  This is a
strong argument, but it is not conclusive.  The
change might have been accomplished in a less
violent manner and still have conditioned the appearance of the moral reaction.  As long as the
pressure of the primal father was felt the hostile
feelings against him were justified and repentance at these feelings had to wait for another opportunity.  Of as little validity is the second objection, that everything derived from the ambivalent relation to the father, namely taboos, and
rules of sacrifice, is characterized by the highest
seriousness and by complete reality.  The cere-

[97] See Chapter III.

monials and inhibitions of compulsion neurotics
exhibit this characteristic too and yet they go back
to a merely psychic reality, to resolution and not
to execution. We must beware of introducing
the contempt for what is merely thought or
wished which characterizes our sober world where
there are only material values, into the world of
primitive man and the neurotic, which is full of
inner riches only.

We face a decision here which is really not
easy. But let us begin by acknowledging that
the difference which may seem fundamental to
others does not, in our judgment, touch the most
important part of the subject. If wishes and
impulses have the full value of fact for primitive
man, it is for us to follow such a conception intelligently instead of correcting it according to
our standard. But in that case we must scruti-
nize more closely the prototype of the neurosis
itself which is responsible for having raised this
doubt. It is not true that compulsion neurotics,
who to-day are under the pressure of over-moral-
ity, defend themselves only against the psychic
reality of temptations and punish themselves for
impulses which they have only felt. A piece of
historic reality is also involved; in their childhood
these persons had nothing but evil impulses and
as far as their childish impotence permitted they
put them into action. Each of these over-good

persons had a period of badness in his childhood, and a perverse phase as a fore-runner and a premise of the later over morality. The analogy between primitive men and neurotics is therefore much more fundamentally established if we assume that with the former, too, the psychic reality, concerning whose structure there is no doubt, originally coincided with the actual reality, and that primitive men really did what according to all testimony they intended to do.

But we must not let our judgment about primitive men be influenced too far by the analogy with neurotics. Differences must also be taken into account. Of course the sharp division between thinking and doing as we draw it does not exist either with savages or with neurotics. But the neurotic is above all inhibited in his actions, with him the thought is a complete substitute for the deed. Primitive man is not inhibited, the thought is directly converted into the deed, the deed is for him so to speak rather a substitute for the thought, and for that reason I think we may well assume in the case we are discussing, though without vouching for the absolute certainty of the decision, that, "In the beginning was the deed."

**THE END**